IT'S A MATTER OF

LIFE
or
DEATH

WRONG THINKING ABOUT MARRIAGE

LEADS TO DESTRUCTION!

JUDITH A. BRUMBAUGH

Copyright © 1989
by Judith A. Brumbaugh

All rights reserved. No part of this book may be reproduced or transmitted in any form or by any means, electronic or mechanical, without permission in writing from the publisher:

COMMITTEE FOR THE RESTORATION OF THE FAMILY
Box 1342
Oviedo, FL 32765

Library of Congress Catalog Card Number: 89-86047
ISBN 0-9624603-1-1

Illustrator
Ed French

Editor
Judith Shannon

DEDICATION

Dedicated to **Doug** and our children, **Shawn and Mike**

. . . and to parents, who have shown by example, the meaning of a vow and covenant - Reuben & Dorothy Hill, who celebrated their 50th Wedding Anniversary, September 17, 1988.

INTRODUCTION

"In these last days, we must have the Truth of God's Word in every area of our lives. A true Christian can never consider divorce and remarriage (outside of death). But, does the church know the Scriptures relating to this? This book is based and written only on the Truth of God's Word and not man's 'feelings.' Teaching a class of young adults that have desired only God's best for their lives, this book has erased much of man's false teaching and brought them into a deeper understanding of the Scriptures for their future marriages and families."

Andrew and Grace Jorgensen
Ministry to Families
Otto, North Carolina

"If experience is the best teacher, then the author of this book is highly qualified to write on the wickedness of our present judicial system that is programmed to destroy homes and not save them and on the heartache of having one's home and family ripped away while you do everything you can to prevent it. To find a clear resolution to this chaos from God's Word, study this text. It has the answer every Christian must hear."

Pastor Joseph Webb
Calvary Baptist Church
Lake Mary, Florida

FOREWORD

Why is it that we tell small children: "Don't run out into the street; don't put things into the electrical socket; don't pull the pot of hot boiling water over on you"? Isn't it because we love them? Often times, it takes physical restraint to keep children from doing things that will harm or even kill them. Some children respond in obedience to what they are told immediately; others rebel, throw temper tantrums, or get angry at their moms and dads.

Parents who give in to this type of behavior from their children usually find that these individuals as adults are still rebelling against peers, employers, or a mate. A father and mother may even see a child's life lost in a tragic accident stemming from not following the guidelines or precepts "issued" by the parents. We don't normally say to children: "If you feel like that's what you want to do, go ahead. I love you too much to tell you not to run out into the street." We know that **love** involves doing something. It is training children so that they will be aware of harmful acts which if pursued would bring permanent damage. In the primary years, children do not understand so as parents we use other "methods" to convince our offspring that they should obey.

Adults, too, can do things which will harm them. We have seen the statistics on the deaths caused by drunk drivers. Our legislative system has passed laws which make it illegal for people who have been drinking to drive. Likewise, laws have been passed which make it illegal for people to murder and to steal. Does this mean that people no longer do these things? Of course not. Why then have these laws if people continue to commit such acts? We hope that with the governmental regulations a large percentage of the people will be deterred from such behavior because they know that the **wages** of their transgressions could mean imprisonment or even death.

The message of this book is a message of love. It is a message for adults. Like our children, whom we tell not to run into the street because we **know** that they will most likely be killed if they do so; or that they will be scalded if they pull a pan of hot boiling water over on them; or that they will be electrocuted if they stick a sharp object into a light fixture; adults have rules, guidelines, laws, and principles, which if not followed, will lead to unpleasant results. The younger children are, the less likely it is that they will understand why you won't allow them to do what they want to do. Many times it even takes physical restraint to keep them from doing what you know will harm them.

Adults are much the same except on a different level. There are rebellious lifestyles which adults can choose. Some, like children, may not always understand the ramifications of their actions. Others know and will still persist in wrong behavior. Unfortunately, until adults are placed in some type of correctional institution, or until their lives end, their rejection of what is right is often not immediately dealt with. Consequently, they interpret what is wrong as being right.

A book was written many years ago summarizing in human terms the **love** of one person, God. In this book, He teaches by parables, by examples, by sermons, through prophets, teachers, and everyday people like you and me, and by the personal sacrifice of His only Son, Jesus Christ. The crucifixion of God's Son shows the depth of His **love** for us.

Just as each individual is valuable to God, marriage and families are also important to Him. The Lord instituted marriage and recorded this **act** in the book of Genesis. He has spent centuries telling and showing people the true meaning of love worked out in a marriage relationship. He also shows us the repercussions if we violate that relationship. Why does He do this? Because we are His children, and like a loving parent, He does not want us to be destroyed, to suffer hardship, or to bring harm to others. He doesn't tell us these things because He wants to be unkind; but like the parents of children, He desires to show His love for us.

Many of today's churches do not teach the Biblical message regarding the **permanence** of the marriage-covenant and vows. They avoid many of the painful areas related to the breakup of the family, even though it was created because one or both spouses determined by a free-will choice to stop loving his or her mate. Friends of divorced spouses evade talking about the commitment that was made on the wedding day. Why? Their response is often because they say they "love" people too much to be condemning, legalistic, or to "put on" their friends what doesn't seem like what God would expect. Some spouses involved in the breakup of their families respond that they have a "right" to change their minds - that God would want them to be happy.

In studying the Scriptures, however, God repeatedly tells people what they do not want to hear and informs them what would happen if they break His commandments, laws, precepts, or statutes. The purpose of this book is to relate episodes from the lives of people who lived in both New and Old Testament times to show from the Bible how God defines **love** as it is related to marriage and the **wages** involved in not keeping the covenant and vows related to this holy sacrament.

Judith A. Brumbaugh
B.A. Adrian College
MHE University of Georgia

TABLE OF CONTENTS

Chapter 1	THE TROJAN HORSE, HAS IT ENTERED YOUR HOME?	 1
Chapter 2	THE MARRIAGE-COVENANT AND VOWS WHAT DO THEY MEAN?	 12
Chapter 3	WHY DIDN'T JOSEPH HAVE MARY STONED TO DEATH?	 34
Chapter 4	WHAT DID JESUS REALLY SAY TO THE WOMAN AT THE WELL?	 48
Chapter 5	WHY WAS JOHN THE BAPTIST'S HEAD CUT OFF?	 65
Chapter 6	DID DAVID AND BATHSHEBA GET AWAY WITH ADULTERY?	 80
Chapter 7	WHAT WAS HOSEA'S HEARTBREAK?	 104
Chapter 8	WHAT DOES GOD HAVE TO SAY TO THE CHURCHES?	 118
Chapter 9	WHAT DOES OUR GOVERNMENT SAY ABOUT MARRIAGE?	 142
Chapter 10	WHAT IF . . . ?	 172
	BIBLIOGRAPHY	 187

CHAPTER 1
THE TROJAN HORSE
HAS IT ENTERED YOUR HOME?

A walk back in history takes us to 1184 B.C., not long after the end of the Bronze Age, where a legend, thought to have been based on an historical event, has been carried forward to today. Most people recognize the Trojan Horse and the tragedy behind its surface meaning: a city destroyed because of the acceptance of a deceitful gift - a magnificent, huge, hand-carved wooden horse. What was inside this beautifully wrapped "package" were armed, trained, war soldiers just awaiting the time of their release through a secret door in the bottom side of the horse. This perilous gift was pulled through the protective city gates by the citizenry of Troy, a city which up until this time had been impenetrable by any enemy.

Troy was a city on the coast of Asia Minor. The king of Troy, Priam, had a son named Paris who was often sent to other cities as ambassador for good will and trade. Paris was gifted not only with talents to fulfill his diplomatic assignments, but he possessed charisma and had a strong influence over people. One city to which he traveled was Sparta, a city in Greece. The king of Sparta, Menelaus, had a wife, Helen, who was acclaimed to be the most beautiful woman in the whole world. Paris, of course, also was aware of this attractive woman. He decided he wanted to have her as his wife. Helen was lured by him and became part of a kidnaping scheme. Paris quickly won favor with many of those in King Menelaus' court and conspired with them to execute the plan to kidnap Helen. When the time was right, the plot was carried out and the beautiful lady of Greece sailed away with Paris back to Troy.

King Menelaus was despondent, hurt, and angry

for quite some time. When he recovered he resolved to get his wife back. Since Troy was well known as an impregnable city with its huge protective wall around its entire circumference, Menelaus joined forces with the chieftains and warriors of Greece to assemble optimum talent and strength for the planned battle.

A ten-year war ensued outside the walls of Troy, employing the best leadership and battle techniques known, but the warriors could not penetrate the Trojan wall. At last, however, King Menelaus' forces came up with a strategy whereby the Trojans would take part in their own self-destruction, a plan for devastation "from within" based upon the innate weakness of man - a desire to possess those things which he does not presently have called lust.

The new battle plan was put into practice. We now find the Greeks busily constructing a gigantic, beautiful wooden horse, hollow inside to house an army of soldiers. The horse, once completed, was rolled to the main gate of the city of Troy. Menelaus' warriors then pretended to sail home to abandon their ten-year quest for the return of King Menelaus' wife.

Conversation inside the walls of Troy heightened. "We have won! They could not conquer us but . . . what could this strange horse be? It's so beautifully hand crafted with the finest of wood. Surely someone should investigate!"

The Trojans came outside the gates of the city to get a closer look at this "strange animal." A Greek soldier had been left behind to tell them that the horse was an offering to the goddess Athena. Believing that the horse would bring them good luck, the Trojans decided to drag this welcomed gift inside the city gates. They found, however, that it was so large that they could not get it through the gates, so they proceeded to tear down part of their protective wall in order to bring this "omen" of good luck inside. That night, the Trojans had a great celebration lasting into the early hours of the morning. All watch guards along the wall likewise left their posts and joined the party. It was then that the Greek warriors opened the trap door and slid down a rope from under the belly of the horse. Their comrades waiting outside the walls were beckoned and the

total siege of the city took place.

What a price to pay for the lust of one man and woman! Has man learned from past events, or does history continue to repeat itself with new faces? From the days of Adam and Eve, there has been historical repetition of this innate weakness in man, the lust of the eye. Episode after episode of it has been told repeatedly for man to study and learn with its accompanying repercussions: **"Be not deceived . . . whatsoever a man soweth, that shall he also reap."*** (Gal. 6:7)

What is lust?

Lust is a broad term including any evil desire. In this text the emphasis is upon sexual lust, but the reader should be aware that the term applies to other sins. Lust generally enters the body through the eyes and when "processed" by an unrighteous heart will manifest itself in sin by the flesh (body). The lust demonstrated by the lives in this chapter includes sexual lust by Paris and an evil desire to become all-knowing gods by Adam and Eve. Both examples were very costly, not only for those directly involved but for other **innocent lives** that became affected immediately and for centuries thereafter. The Bible refers to the cost of such actions as the **wages** of sin. Rarely is sin contained within the immediate people committing it. The ramifications are far-reaching and for many result in eternal death, or as the Scriptures tell us: **"The wages of sin is death; but the gift of God is eternal life through Jesus Christ our Lord."** (Rom. 6:23)

Some people are consumed by the desire for riches; for others, it may be a drug, gluttony, sexual activity, or some

---

***"Bold highlighting enclosed by quotations marks"** indicates quotes from the King James version of the Bible. Biblical references are used with punctuation as it appears within this translation. Underlining is added by the author for emphasis.

type of power. All of the above in proper balance and within Biblical context are not evil. They become lustful when man perverts them by rejecting standards set by God and replacing righteousness with misguided principles set in place by man in his effort to **benefit self** - often at the expense of others. Some of the many Biblical references describing lust and its dangers are given below:

> "So I gave them up unto their own heart's <u>lust</u>: and they walked in their own counsels." (Psa. 81:12)

> "<u>Lust</u> not after her beauty in thine heart; neither let her take thee with her eyelids." (Pro. 6:24)

> "But I say unto you, That whosoever looketh on a woman to <u>lust</u> after her hath committed adultery with her already in his heart." (Matt. 5:28)

> "And the cares of this world, and the deceitfulness of riches, and the <u>lusts</u> of other things entering in, choke the word, and it becometh unfruitful." (Mark 4:19)

> "That ye put off concerning the former conversation of the old man, which is corrupt according to the deceitful <u>lusts</u>." (Eph. 4:22)

> "For the time will come when they will not endure sound doctrine; but after their own <u>lusts</u> shall they heap to themselves teachers, having itching ears; And they shall turn away their ears from the truth, and shall be turned unto fables." (2 Tim. 4:3,4)

> "But every man is tempted, when he is drawn away of his own <u>lust</u>, and enticed. Then when lust hath conceived, it bringeth forth sin: and <u>sin</u>, when it is finished, <u>bringeth forth death</u>." (Jas. 1:14)

We must daily search our lives for any Trojan Horse

which might entice us because of its seeming beauty. Sin is not normally packaged with a "danger, keep out" sign. It looks good in the beginning, but . . . **"when lust hath conceived, it bringeth forth sin: and sin, when it is finished, bringeth forth death."** Indeed, the **wages** of sin can be very costly!

What was the "wages" of Adam and Eve's lust?

Let's take a look at another story about lust but this time one recorded in the Bible and concerning the desire to supersede God. This takes us to the garden of Eden, a paradise of peace, abundance, and total provision for mankind. We are told in Genesis 1:28 that man had dominion over every living thing that "moveth" upon the earth as well as over the fish of the sea. Yes, in the garden of Eden there was an almost infinite supply of everything needed by man. Adam and Eve would have probably qualified for the "Lifestyles of the Rich and Famous" in today's economy! Only one limitation in all of creation was placed upon them: **"And the Lord God commanded the man saying, Of every tree of the garden thou mayest freely eat: But of the tree of the knowledge of good and evil, thou shalt not eat of it: for in the day that thou eatest thereof thou shalt surely die."** (Gen. 2:16,17) Along with our gift of free will, God sets before every man "trials of obedience." These are not to make man sin but to show him what truly is inside (in his heart); that he may, by God's grace, rid himself of this guile: **"Let no man say when he is tempted, I am tempted of God: for God cannot be tempted with evil, neither tempteth he any man: But every man is tempted, when he is drawn away of his own lust, and enticed. Then when lust hath conceived, it bringeth forth sin: and sin, when it is finished, bringeth forth death."** (Jas. 1:13-15)

Even here in this garden of paradise and abundance was lurking around the corner that old enemy, lust, clothed by deception. The first breaking down of Adam and Eve's "wall" was for someone to lure part of this family off to the side without the other half. The serpent, in the initial part of his subtle plan, came solely to Eve. He then cleverly misquoted only a small portion of what had been commanded: **"Yea, hath God said, Ye shall not eat of every tree of the garden? And the woman said unto the serpent, We may eat of the fruit of the trees of the garden: But of the fruit of the tree which is in the midst of the garden, God hath said, Ye shall not eat of it, neither shall ye touch it, lest ye die."** (Gen. 3:2,3)

With Eve talking and perhaps reflecting on why God would make what seemed like such a ridiculous restriction, the serpent realized that she didn't "know" the Word as well as he. When she responded, Eve misquoted the Word: **"neither shall ye touch it."** The serpent took advantage of her lack of knowledge in his reply by knowingly misquoting the Word: **"Ye shall not surely die: For God doth know that in the day ye eat thereof, then your eyes shall be opened and ye shall be as gods, knowing good and evil."** Eve's ignorance of Truth was established and now her lust was fed and encouraged by approval from someone trained in deception. She responds with a newly found awareness and a free-will choice to rebel against the Word of God: **"And when the woman saw that the tree was good for food, and that it was pleasant to the eyes, and a tree to be desired to make one wise, she took of the fruit thereof, and did eat, and gave also unto her husband with her: and he did eat."** (Gen. 3:6) When man sins the first time, his conscience is pricked; he knows that he does wrong. This, too, happened with Adam and Eve. The key, however, is how man deals with his conscience. **"And the eyes of them both were opened."** (Gen. 3:7) **". . . their conscience also bearing witness, and their thoughts the mean while accusing or else excusing one another."** (Rom. 2:15)

Adam and Eve knew they had committed a terrible sin but tried to conceal it from God. No one, however, can hide anything from an all-seeing God. The Lord asked not why they had sinned, but **"Hast thou eaten of the tree whereof I commanded thee that thou shouldest not eat?"** Each tried to shift the blame. Adam answered, **"The woman whom thou gavest to be with me, she gave me of the tree, and I did eat."** It, however, was not Eve but Adam to whom God gave His directive: **"And the Lord God commanded man, saying, Of** every tree of the garden thou mayest freely eat: but of the tree of the knowledge of good and evil, thou shalt not eat of it . . ." (Gen. 2:27) This was prior to God's taking of woman from man and <u>creating the institution of marriage</u>. "And the Lord God caused a deep sleep to fall upon Adam, and he slept: and he took one of his ribs, and closed up the flesh instead thereof; And the rib, which the Lord God had taken from man, made he a woman, and brought her unto the man. And Adam said, <u>This is now bone of my bones, and flesh of my flesh: she shall be called Woman</u> . . ." (Gen. 2:23)

As head of the household God made man responsible to teach his wife (and family) the commands of the Lord, but in so doing, He did not "excuse" woman from repercussions of violating God's laws. ("**But I would have you know, that the head of every man is Christ; and the head of the woman is the man; and the head of Christ is God . . . Husbands, love your wives,** <u>even as Christ</u> **also loved the church, and gave himself for it; That he might** <u>sanctify and cleanse</u> **it with the washing of water** <u>by the word</u> **. . . ye husbands, dwell with them** (wives) **according to knowledge . . . being heirs together of the grace of life.**" (I Cor. 11:3; Eph. 5:25,26; I Peter 3:7) "**Fathers, provoke not your children to wrath: but bring them up in the nurture and admonition of the Lord.**" (Eph. 6:4)

Adam and Eve chose to reject what God's word said. Each had different excuses, but both were held accountable. When taken aside by "the world," Eve saw how enticing sin was. Her response to God was: "**The serpent beguiled me, and I did eat.**" (Gen. 3:13) "**For Adam was first formed, then Eve. And Adam** <u>was</u> <u>not</u> <u>deceived</u>**, but the woman being deceived was in the transgression.**" (I Tim. 2:13,14)

Like sin today, it was so with Adam and Eve. There was a sowing and reaping. Their rebellion affected not only their lives but generations thereafter. With their sin and "fall," spiritual and physical death were introduced into the human race. To the serpent God said:

1. "**upon thy belly shall thou go, and dust shalt thou eat all the days of thy life;**
2. **and I will put enmity between thee and the woman and between thy seed and her seed;**

3. it shall bruise thy head, and thou shalt bruise his heel." (Gen. 3:14,15)

Notice above that there was a physical change, a relational change, and a prophesy. The serpent was from this day forth, for his part in man's apostasy, to be deprived of his limbs, and condemned henceforth to crawl upon the earth on his belly. He apparently was not that way previously. He was "cast" in Genesis 3:1 as **"more subtil than any beast of the field."** And as the conversation in verse three indicates, the serpent and man enjoyed some level of communication and a relationship of a more positive nature than the repulsive image envisioned today when reminded of a snake. The third part of this proclamation was the initial prophesy of the birth and death of Jesus Christ. (See Chapter Three for a discussion of points two and three.)

The Lord continued in verses 16 through 18 to show man, Adam and Eve, what "he" would have to reap from the results of the lust in the heart. This included:

1. pain in childbirth
2. toil upon the earth
3. and physical death

"Unto the woman he said, I will greatly multiply thy sorrow and thy conception; in sorrow thou shalt bring forth children; and thy desire shall be to thy husband, and he shall rule over thee. And unto Adam he said, Because thou hast hearkened unto the voice of thy wife, and hast eaten of the tree, of which I commanded thee, saying, Thou shalt not eat of it: cursed is the ground for thy sake; in sorrow shalt thou eat of it all the days of thy life; thorns also and thistles shall it bring forth to thee; and thou shalt eat the herb of the field: in the sweat of thy face shalt thou eat bread, <u>till thou return unto the ground</u>; for out of it wast thou taken: for dust thou art, and unto dust shalt thou return." (Gen. 3:16-19)

Through this well-known Biblical account, God set forth "in the beginning," precepts and principles which man can choose to obey or disobey with the accompanying blessings or curses. These have <u>never</u> been rescinded by God; only "<u>provisions</u>" for dealing with rebellion have been "<u>allowed</u>"

by man. For example, we find in Mark, Chapter Ten, Jesus talking with the Pharisees who were trying to excuse divorce and wanting to trap Jesus into agreeing with the same. They told Jesus that "**Moses suffered to write a bill of divorcement, and to put her away.**" Jesus wasted no time in not only correcting their implication that divorce had been given a stamp of approval but referred them back to the original (Genesis 2:4) which has never been set aside by God. "**And Jesus answered and said unto them, For the hardness of your heart he** (Moses) **wrote you this precept. But from the beginning of the creation God made them male and female . . . they are no more twain, but one flesh . . . whosoever shall put away his wife, and marry another, committeth adultery against her. And if a woman shall put away her husband, and be married to another, she committeth adultery.**" (Mark 10:5-12)

In applying the Word to personal lives, man must first study the Word for himself to establish a Biblical basis for daily life and then continually make application based upon these premises:

1. What God's Word says must be measured by what God commands and not how man twists It to satisfy or appease changing morality.

2. What God pronounces rarely comes to pass immediately; it sometimes takes days, months, years, or even centuries for man to reap blessings or curses from obedience or rebellion.

3. God's Word (The Bible) is not changed because of man's transgressions, laws, or the passage of time. "**For I am the Lord, I change not.**" "**Jesus Christ the same yesterday, and today, and for ever.**" (Mal. 3:6; Heb. 13:8)

4. It is God who established the institution of marriage and the principles by which man and woman must "live and work together in this life so that in the world to come they may have life everlasting." (See page 33.)

God said: "**for in the day that thou eatest thereof thou shalt surely die.**" Deceived through lust, rebellion, and sometimes ignorance of Biblical veracity, man changes Truth into apostasy. He says, "Ye shall **not surely die.** Do what will satisfy your desires and make you happy. Follow that which society, the government, the 'church' says is okay, even if it is in opposition to what God's Word says." It is true that Adam and Eve did not die immediately . . . but some 1,000 years later, this couple did die having "toiled" upon the land. They had been forever banished from a paradise never since equaled in opulence, majesty, or pleasure upon this earth. Even today, Genesis Three has not been totally fulfilled, but we are a part of the "toil" of this earth. The serpent slithers along the ground on his belly; Christ was born of the <u>seed of woman</u>; and man, whether Christian or non-Christian, whether saved or not saved, is reminded of the "revelation" of God's Word Who walked on this very earth. In an act as mundane as writing a check or referring to a calendar, man is daily reminded of the birth of Christ - the numerics of this universal document, the calendar, being based upon the birth of Christ!

And so, the **wages** of sin continue even unto today . . . "**And the serpent said unto the woman, <u>ye shall not surely die</u>;**" "Let me break through your **wall**," says lust, "surely you will not be punished if you disobey God's word!"

CHAPTER 2
THE MARRIAGE-COVENANT AND VOWS
WHAT DO THEY MEAN?

To say "I do" or "I will" as a commitment of love to another person encompasses two of the shortest, simplest words in man's vocabulary. Ironically, man probably has less understanding of the far-reaching ramifications involved in this pledge than any other voluntary, declarative statement he ever has or ever will make.

A marriage ceremony is an event almost everyone has attended at least once in his/her lifetime. Many deem this ritual as a civil or religious relationship between two people and the state or some religious group. Because they believe that the government or some church official marries them, spouses will many years later go to one of the above to rescind agreements made on the wedding day through divorce or annulment.

The problem here is that man fails to understand that marriage is not an institution that humans originated. Marriage is an **act** performed by God who **creates** something new - a one-flesh union. The state/church only recognizes this union, the former merely giving this "unit" sanction to enter into legal agreements as a partnership.

Marriage is a **covenant** between God and the bride and groom. This relationship becomes a permanent, indissoluble bond until the death of one of the parties to this agreement. The words exchanged during the wedding ceremony have a more far-reaching significance than most participants realize.

An example of the verbal commitments made during a wedding ceremony is given on pages 31 through 33. Turn there to read "The Order for the Solemnization of Matrimony." Several areas of that document have been highlighted with **bold lettering and underlining, followed by a subscript**$_1$, $_2$, $_3$, etc. These are key concepts that prospective husbands and wives should thoroughly study before entering into a marriage ceremony. Those who are already married may need to carefully review the covenant and vows to which they previously agreed. As the above-accented areas of "The Order for the Solemnization of Matrimony" are discussed within this text, they will likewise be emphasized as outlined above.

Who created the institution of marriage?

In most marriage ceremonies, man publicly acknowledges, before witnesses, vows that he agrees to uphold. This is done prior to entering into a covenant with God. Through this **covenant,**$_3$ God <u>**mysteriously**</u> changes two people into one flesh for the rest of their days here on this earth. God has made this awesome, <u>permanent bond</u> indissoluble this side of death.

The record of the creation of this institution and the rules by which it is governed are given in the Bible. (Biblical references in this text will be indicated by "**bold highlighting and quotation marks.**"*) The Bible is the sole authority regarding marriage. Christians and non-Christians alike are held accountable to what the Bible states is Truth. This means that it doesn't matter whether you are a Christian or not, the <u>first</u> time you <u>both</u> enter into a marriage-covenant with a person of the opposite sex, God will hold you responsible for the covenant you make <u>until</u> either you or your spouse dies even though you may not fully understand that to which you have sworn. "**As I live, saith the Lord, <u>every knee</u> shall bow to me, and every tongue shall confess to God. So then <u>every one</u> of us shall give an account of himself to God.**" (Rom. 14:11,12) "**When thou vowest a vow unto God, defer not to pay it; for he hath no pleasure in fools: pay that which thou hast vowed. Suffer**

---

*The King James version will be used for Biblical references. The author will add underlining for emphasis.

not thy mouth to cause thy flesh to sin; neither say thou before the angel, that it was an error: wherefore should God be angry at thy voice and destroy the work of thine hands?"** (Ecc. 5:4,6)

When you are issued a driver's license, you agree to obey all of the laws regarding our highways. Because you do not understand them or know them does not excuse you from obeying them. Likewise, with marriage, you may not "know" what the Bible says, but God holds you accountable. It is an open book test. You choose whether to study it or not. And as in other "infractions" of God's laws, **"My people are destroyed for lack of knowledge: because thou hast rejected knowledge, I will also reject thee."** (Hosea 4:6)

Once both parties repeat the words, "I _____, take thee, _____, to be my wedded husband/wife," they have entered into an irreversible permanent bond that makes them one flesh via God's institution of marriage. This happens by virtue of what God calls a **covenant** with Him. In Mark 10:8, God has left a permanent record for man regarding this institution of marriage: **"And they twain shall be one flesh."** God, Himself, re-emphasizes this fact by immediately restating the principle so that there will be no misunderstanding: **"so then they are no more twain, but one flesh."** Most people are not as familiar with the Scriptures as they are with the "intent" of the marriage-covenant and vows. Both, however, strongly show the permanence of marriage unless man determines to pervert either by purposely twisting the wording or omitting portions designed to confirm God's commands regarding His institution.

It is indeed tragic that man does not recognize God's part in creating marriage and man's responsibility in preserving it. In his ignorance, and/or rebellion, man uses misguided philosophies based on false premises in attempting to dissolve what God says is indissoluble. These false doctrines are based upon wrong teachings regarding the question of who or what act it is that changes two people who come to the altar into a permanent one-flesh bond. Is it the officiating person who says, "I now pronounce you husband and wife"? Is it the act of sex which man says "consummates" a marriage? An affirmative answer to either of the above is incorrect. Together we will search for the Biblical answers to the following questions:

1. Who is it that marries a man and woman?
2. What do the marriage-covenant and vows mean?
3. What is love?

Who is it that marries a man and woman?

At the moment that two people make their marriage-covenant, the moment when they say, "I, _____, take thee, _____, to be my wedded husband/wife," a **miracle** occurs that man does not physically see. These two people are **mysteriously** made "one." Like the conception of a child, wherein the parents do not actually witness the creation nor at that instant feel any differently, a bride and groom are not physically aware that they have become one flesh. However, if properly nourished by God's principles, this "seed," whether it be the birth of a child or that of a marriage, will grow and develop into something beautiful. Unfortunately, however, most husbands and wives never experience the fulfillment available within the confines of the institution of marriage.

Reflect for a moment on two of the underlined words above:

mystery: anything that is kept secret or remains unexplained or unknown; any truth unknowable except by divine revelation

miracle: an effect or extraordinary event in the physical world which surpasses all known human or natural powers and is ascribed to a supernatural cause

It is important that you not hurry over these concepts. This miracle, the **mystical union**,$_2$ is the key to understanding the significance of the institution of marriage. This is God's **covenant** between Him and the man and woman coming before Him to be united. The Truth which most people miss is that God is the creator and controller of this **covenant-creation** rather than man.

This "creation" of one flesh happens as soon as you

partake in a ceremony and commit to a marriage-covenant. God is the witness and in so being makes you one flesh at that very moment. The "**new being**" is not created when someone says, "In the name of the Father, and the Son, and the Holy Ghost, I pronounce you husband and wife." The person officiating is only acknowledging for all of those present that **GOD** has made two people one. It is not the pastor, or the priest, or the rabbi, or the justice of peace who creates this oneness. It is Almighty God. Clergymen and representatives of the state only officiate at the ceremony. They neither make you one flesh nor can they ever dissolve what God has created.

It has been established that God is the one who makes a bride and groom one flesh - what man calls marriage. **God instituted marriage**$_1$, and very much approves of it in a Biblical context. He lets us know that this was not just an Old Testament custom, but something He established as an on-going universal law. Man today knows in his heart that marriage is for life, but like the Pharisees of Jesus' day, he will continue asking if there isn't some excuse to divorce a mate. This may seem like a negative concern for those reading this text who are not considering divorce, but our nation has one of the highest divorce rates in the entire world.

"But," you say, "this would never happen to me. I love my fiancee' or spouse too much." Most marriages begin this way. Please, however, stop and ponder this statistic: over 50 percent of American marriages go through a divorce proceeding. This means that more than every other marriage has and will fall prey to destruction. The purpose of this text is to make people aware of false thinking about marriage so that the Trojan Horse, No-fault Divorce, can be stopped; that the home you have established or are about to establish will have an impenetrable wall around it to keep out any influence that may invite a divorce.

The Pharisees mentioned above were Biblical scholars. They knew what the Word said. They, however, came to Jesus with the purpose of trying to trap Him into indicating that divorce was acceptable. Jesus knew that their motive was wrong. Their encounter is recorded in Matthew 19. **"The**

Pharisees also came unto him, tempting him, and saying unto him, Is it lawful for a man to put away his wife for every cause?" Instead of responding with excuses or options or even discussing why they might want a divorce, Jesus told them where every person should look for answers regarding marriage - to the Bible. He told them that they would know <u>if they read the Word</u>, being aware of course, that they very well knew what the Word said. "**Have ye not read, that <u>he</u> which made them at the beginning made them <u>male</u> <u>and</u> <u>female</u> . . . and the twain shall be one flesh? Wherefore they are <u>no more</u> twain, but one flesh. What therefore <u>God hath joined together</u>, let not man put asunder.**" (Matt. 19:4-6)

Going back to the first chapter of Genesis, God said, "**Let us make man in our image . . . So God created man in his own image, in the image of God created he him: <u>male and female</u> created he them.**" Man was first formed "**out of the dust of the ground . . . and man became a <u>living soul</u>.**" After the garden of Eden was prepared, "**the Lord God caused a deep sleep to fall upon Adam, and he slept: and he took one of his ribs, and closed up the flesh instead thereof; And the rib, which the Lord God had taken from man, made he a woman, <u>and brought her unto the man</u>.**"*

In human terms, this joining "**they twain shall be one flesh**," was symbolized in the creation of woman. Eve was taken from Adam's side so that he could not put her away. If he did, it would be like putting away a part of himself and thus contradicting the very proof of her creation - a oneness that could not be more indissoluble - a <u>bond</u> closer than that between parents and children. A man's children

---

*Parents correctly follow Biblical procedure today when the father brings the bride to the groom during the wedding ceremony. As "head" of the family, the father represents both the father and mother and is showing the consent of the one-flesh. Exercised here is the Biblical principle that the children should have their parents' consent before entering into a marriage-covenant and the parents' responsibility in giving such.

are pieces of himself, but his wife <u>is</u> himself. When Adam lost his rib to Eve he lost no strength. Instead he gained a lifetime help-mate with this his companion and the wife of his covenant. By turning to the fifth chapter of Ephesians, you will see another restatement of this indissoluble covenant: **"So ought men to love their wives as their own bodies. He that loveth his <u>wife</u> loveth <u>himself</u>. For no man ever yet hated <u>his</u> <u>own</u> <u>flesh</u>: but nourisheth and cherisheth it . . . For we are members of his body of his flesh, and of his bones. <u>For this cause</u> shall a man leave his father and mother, and shall be joined unto his wife, and they <u>two shall be one flesh</u>.** The nature of the marriage-covenant is a union of persons.

Marriage is between one man and one woman for a lifetime upon this earth, and the relation between the two is to be as unto one's own body. Adam repeated a much shortened version of today's marriage ceremony. It apparently was not necessary for him to repeat the vows but only to affirm that he understood the meaning of the marriage-covenant, this "creation" from the hands of God between God and Adam and Eve. **"And Adam said, This is <u>now</u> bone of my bones, and flesh of my flesh."** (Gen. 2:23) <u>This is God's original marriage ceremony</u>.

God teaches us that He made one female for one male. He could have made many wives for Adam, but He did not: **"and did not he make one? Yet had he the residue of the spirit. And wherefore one? That he might seek a godly seed."** (Mal. 2:15) God certainly could have made more wives, but instead He says that every man should have his own wife, <u>only one</u>, that they might live in chaste and holy love under the directions and restraints of Divine law. When this male and female, Adam and Eve, were joined together in holy marriage, the law of marriage stated that a man must **"<u>leave</u> his father and mother, <u>and</u> cleave to his wife."** (Gen. 2:24)

Husband and wife joined together by the ordinance of God are not to be put asunder by any ordinance of man, including that of the government through divorce or that of the church through annulment. These institutions <u>officiate</u> at ceremonies. They are **not** God and are <u>not</u> a part of the marriage-covenant: "**the Lord** hath been **witness** between thee and the wife of thy youth . . . thy companion, and **wife of thy covenant.**" (Mal. 2:14)

Corruption which creeps into any ordinance of God must be purged by going back to its origin in Scripture. Adulterated versions must be eliminated. Truth, as stated by God, is "**from the beginning**" and not in the permissions, tolerations, and allowances given to rebellious, sinful man.

The Lord repeatedly commands man not to touch His institution - marriage. This He does not only as we are reminded at the end of the marriage ceremony,[9] but also as explicitly stated in God's Word: "**Wherefore they are no more twain, but one flesh. What therefore God hath joined together, let not man put asunder.**" (Matt. 19:6) This same warning is repeated numerous times throughout the Scriptures, both in the Old and New Testaments. The difference between the two accounts is the specific warning God gives to man in the New Testament to not attempt to dissolve what He has created. Man not understanding the "creation" of one person through marriage, often goes to the courts or the church to try to dissolve or annul God's creation with a man-made "device," divorce.

Consider one more analogy regarding this most important principle, the permanence of marriage. Man nor man's institutions can no more dissolve this "creation" than can they "dissolve" a son or daughter born from the physical union of this man and woman. In Genesis 2:24, God simply records " . . . **and they shall be one flesh.**" Flesh and bone indicate a relationship closer than that of your children, yet when man obtains a divorce in our courts, he refers to these one-flesh mates as ex-spouses. Oddly, it should seem that he does not call the children created from this union ex-children. Nor are the grandparents labeled ex-grandparents, or aunts and uncles, ex-aunts and ex-uncles. It seems irrational that the two people who have created the kinship **bond** and without whom no one would be related, are now being "Xed" out! No . . . the children are still the children, the grandparents are still the grandparents . . . and the two spouses are still husband and wife as God has supernaturally in His **mystical union**[2]

19

made them <u>one</u> bone and flesh.

"But," you say, "people get divorced every day, so God must allow it." People also murder, steal, and get drunk every day. Should we likewise rationalize these sins? Hopefully, we do not. Man has a free will, but there is a sowing and reaping process. One day, there will be a price to pay for unrepented sin. The warnings are throughout the Bible. Yes, man can divorce and make another agreement with a different partner. God will "allow" him to do this, but what happens to those who die as murderers, as thieves, as alcoholics? The Scriptures clearly explain. Likewise, what happens to those who die in a sexual relationship of which God does not approve, such as homosexuality, or prostitution, or adultery? **"They which do such things shall not inherit the kingdom of God."** (Gal. 5:21) It is indeed a most unwise decision to purposely rebel against God's commands. This includes not only those who initiate such behavior but also those who make it their profession or habit to encourage or assist such actions. **"But whoso shall offend one of these little ones which believe in me, it were better for him that a millstone were hanged about his neck, and that he were drowned in the depth of the sea."** (Matt. 18:6)

Let's now consider the question, "Is it the act of sex which 'consummates' a marriage?" It is important to understand that sex is not a part of the marriage-covenant: <u>it is a **privilege** that is derived from it</u>.

First of all, if sex marries or "unmarries" people, there would be no such thing as pre- or post-marital sex which God considers sin. Prostitutes perform many of these acts every day, but these do not marry them to their illicit partners nor does it "unmarry" the spouse involved in immoral behavior. Sex outside the bonds of marriage is sin whether it be an act of **fornication** <u>between two unmarried persons</u> or adultery. **Adultery** as defined in the Bible is an act between two persons one of whom God considers to be married to someone not a party to the illicit act. There are many people who through sickness and physical infirmities, imprisonment, or war cannot perform the conjugal "rights" of marriage. These facts, however, do not "unmarry" them. Man, however, uses this kind of irrational reasoning when one of the marriage partners has an affair. He says that adultery is "Scriptural grounds for divorce." He implies that sin dissolves a one-flesh bond. Immoral behavior whether it be sexual or any other type such as murder, lying, or stealing does not create or destroy a marriage-covenant. If illicit sexual union between two people married or "unmarried" them, then it would be impossible to sin if you committed fornication or adultery. Instead of sinning you would be getting married or divorced with God's approval! No, illicit sex neither marries nor "unmarries" those who participate in it. Adultery is one of several sins that without repentance (turning from this behavior) leads to eternal death; it does not, however, dissolve a marriage-covenant.

God clearly defines the penalty for adultery: "**Know ye not that the unrighteous shall not inherit the kingdom of God? Be not deceived: neither fornicators, nor idolaters, nor adulterers . . . shall inherit the kingdom of God.**" (I Cor. 6:9,10) "**Marriage is honorable in all, and the bed undefiled: but whoremongers and adulterers God will judge.**" (Heb. 13:4) He likewise clearly defines adultery, so that man will not have to guess or have any gray areas concerning this sin: "**Whosoever shall put away his wife, and marry another, committeth adultery against her. And if a woman shall put away her husband, and be married to another, she committeth adultery.**" (Mark 10:11,12) The point at which a relationship is considered adultery is not the divorce. It is the marriage to an illicit partner, a lustful desire in your heart for someone not your mate, or the physical sexual relationship outside the bond of one's marriage.

Jesus discussed the only "holy union" sexual privilege; that is, between two people, a man and a woman who are married the first time in His sight, and neither has any other living one-flesh partner. (Mark 10:6-9) Note that as long as a person has another living spouse and determines to concurrently be married to a second, or third, or fourth spouse, that person, in God's eyes, "**shall be called an adulteress.**" "If **while her husband liveth, she be married** to another man, she shall be called an adulteress." (Rom. 7:3) Man tries to appease his conscience and say that this sin is okay, that he can "masque" it by going through another marriage ceremony with the illicit partner, but he cannot deceive God.

The permanence of marriage should be apparent. "**Whosoever**" includes everyone, Christian and non-Christian, those who believe and obey the Word as well as those who do not. God doesn't allude to those who divorce and marry another spouse as husband and wife but as people who are living in adultery. "**Whosoever shall put away his wife, and marry another, committeth adultery against her. And if a woman shall put away her husband, and be married to another, she committeth adultery.**" (Mark 10:2-12) The two from the wedding day forth are united so long as ye both shall live. Any interim marriage, according to the Scriptures, is a sin called adultery. "**If, while her husband liveth, she be married to another man, she shall be called an adulteress.**" (Rom. 7:3)

Yes, this is indeed one of the most serious commitments you will make; it is a lifetime commitment - not the farce that television has made of it and that man has mirrored in daily lifestyles. Wedding vows can be prostituted into heresy by changing them; but if you enter into God's institution with another person of the opposite sex, **the** "rule" book, the Bible, not man, is the final word.

You can build into the vows that if the marriage doesn't go the way you would like it, you can scrap it and find somebody else, but you can only "get away" with that in man's court. One day, whether Christian or non-Christian, whether saved or not saved, you will stand in God's "court," and "**whoremongers and adulterers God will judge.**" The time to examine what the Word says is before marriage, not twenty years from then when society, not God, says it's okay to have an affair; it's okay to have a "mid-life crisis" and discard a lifetime mate; it's okay to do what makes you happy! But . . . God's word disagrees. He calls it prostitution, harlotry, adultery, rebellion, SIN: "**whoso committeth adultery . . . destroyeth his own soul.**" (Pro. 6:32) If you enter into a marriage-covenant with someone of the opposite sex, know that it is a serious matter.

What do the marriage-covenant and vows mean?

The verbal affirmations that are spoken during a marriage ceremony are short and simple, just two words in each declarative statement, "I do" and "I will." Once uttered in a wedding ceremony, two people <u>are</u> one <u>and</u> agree to uphold what God has established within the institution of marriage. Take a moment to study the definitions of these words:

do: to create, form, or bring into being;
to complete, bring about; to effect;
to serve; to execute, accomplish
to finish or be finished

will: about or going to; disposed or willing to; the faculty of conscious and especially of <u>deliberate action</u>; the power of control the mind has over its own actions; power of choosing one's own actions; to decide or determine

Yes, simple little words, but power-packed! Perhaps, they should be packaged and labeled with a warning such as is dynamite: "Handle carefully; extremely dangerous; use only with caution." Or as man is reminded in Ecclesiastes 5:4-6: **"When thou vowest a vow unto God, defer not to pay it; for he hath no pleasure in fools . . . neither say thou before the angel, that it was an error: wherefore should God be angry at thy voice, and destroy the work of thine hands?"**

Again, we need to reference the marriage-covenant and vows, given on pages 31 through 33, specifically subscript$_4$. This section clearly reminds man what the duration of the marriage commitment is **"from this day forward . . . <u>so long as ye both shall live</u>,"**$_4$ a seemingly simple, easy-to-understand statement. On the wedding day, friends, relatives, church and government officials don't tell the bride and groom that it is just their interpretation that they are making a lifetime commitment. No, the meaning of "until death do us part," "in the beginning" of the marriage relationship needs no explanation. It's only after many

23

years when troubles enter the home that then man tries to add his heresy to twist what the covenant and vows very clearly and undeniably say.

Take a close look at what we might call the "exception clause" within the marriage ceremony: **"for better, for worse, for richer, for poorer, in sickness and in health."** This is given on page 32 with the subscript$_5$. Whether these words are specifically spoken or not, they describe what God expects you to honor. We sometimes look too lightly at the extreme contrast embedded within the above commitment. It might be an interesting exercise to stop right now and make a list of every situation that could be enumerated under the following:

FOR BETTER: FOR RICHER: IN HEALTH

My spouse buys me a new car every year.
My spouse is never sick.
My spouse takes me on a vacation every year.
My spouse brings me breakfast in bed on the weekends.
My spouse is attentive to my every need and desire.
My spouse cooks me a gourmet meal once a month.
My spouse provides me with a beautiful wardrobe.
My spouse helps with the children.
My spouse does special things around the house.
My spouse kisses me every morning before leaving for work.
My spouse loves me.

We could continue, but you can add whatever fits your specific circumstances. Now let's build a second list:

FOR WORSE: FOR POORER: IN SICKNESS

My spouse has been physically ill for ten years.
My spouse has been mentally ill for ten years.
My spouse hasn't worked in five years and refuses to look for a job.
My spouse is an alcoholic.
My spouse is a prostitute.

My spouse yells at me all the time.
My spouse refuses to help with the children.
My spouse refuses to have sex with me.
My spouse threatens me with a .357 Magnum.
My spouse is a drug dealer.
My spouse moved me into the street in boxes
 and moved his girlfriend into our home.
I don't love my spouse any more.

Again, we could continue, but you can add whatever fits your specific circumstances. The important thing is to become aware of what happens inside of you when you read the first list as opposed to the second. There would probably be something on the "for worse" list that would make many spouses feel as if they have grounds for divorce. They would be tempted to go to their friends, pastor, rabbi, priest, or attorney to tell them that based on one or more of the above, they feel they cannot live with their spouse any more.

Different responses to the "exception clause" now invoke an entirely new reaction within most people. One-flesh mates will "stick it out" with the first series of events because they are positive, good, kind. With the second series of events, however, man will "bail out" because they are negative, unpleasant, life-threatening. However, from God's point of view and from the commitment tied to the marriage-covenant, there is no difference in regard to the one-flesh bond. In hardship or pleasure we will always be one . . . until death. The separation here is our willingness to accept all that is good, fun, and positive but to reject negative circumstances as something God would not "expect" us to live with. But, once again, this is only man's desire to excuse that to which he has committed. None of those things on the second list are exceptions anywhere in the Bible. If you cannot accept everything on both lists, it is best not to make a marriage-covenant that God considers irrevocable for any reason.

God does, however, **include a provision to live apart from a mate** for those spouses who perhaps face physical abuse or other eminent personal danger. This is given in I Corinthians 7:10,11: "**And unto the married I command, yet not I but the Lord, Let not the wife depart from her husband, But and if she depart, let her remain unmarried, or be reconciled to her husband: and let not the husband put away his wife.**" Note that this "provision" does not open the door for dating or marriage, only for one of two options:

1. to live separate from your spouse, **or**
2. to be reconciled to your one-flesh mate.

God gives **no** permission to marry someone else as long as our one-flesh mate is still living: "**So then if, while her husband liveth, she be married to another man, she shall be called an adulteress; but if her husband be dead, she is free from that law; so that she is no adulteress, though she be married to another man.**" (Rom. 7:3) Again spoken through this same apostle, Paul, this identical set of "statutes" is repeated in I Corinthians 7:39: "**The wife is bound by the law as long as her husband liveth; but if her husband be dead, she is at liberty to be married to whom she will; only in the Lord.**" Yes, God indeed is very serious about His institution. We must "**love and cherish . . . till death us do part.**"$_4$ (Some misguided couples today are changing the vows to read "as long as we both shall love" thinking that they can insert an "exception clause" that will later give them a way out of the marriage. This is false heresy.)

What is love?

Now that the foundation has been laid regarding what marriage is, a lifetime one-flesh bond, and that the institution of marriage is a Divine institution, created and controlled by God, we can lay the proper foundation for living within that institution. Let's look at the most prevalent reason that people give for entering into a marriage-covenant: "I **love**$_7$ him/her and want to live the rest of my life with this person." (See page 31.)

Perhaps it's time to look at that word "love." Nothing is started with higher expectations but fails as regularly as love. With over a 50 percent divorce rate in the United States, it is apparent that man does not understand this simple little word which binds together the commitments of the marriage ceremony. Myth, ignorance, and rebellion surround this word. We hear people say, "I love my car, I love my family, I love my house, I love steak, I love diamonds, I love Charlie Brown, I love my mate." To these, we must add the more uncommon referenced examples. **"Husbands, love your wives, even as Christ also loved the church, and gave himself for it." (Eph. 5:25)** In I Corinthians 13, many references are given to the definition of love: **"beareth all things, endureth all things, never faileth."** I John 2:5 states: **"But whoso keepeth his word, in him verily is the love of God perfected: hereby know we that we are in him."** Here we see love, not as the world defines it, but as God has set the standards for it.

Perhaps, one of the major breakdowns is that man does not know God. God is love. If we don't know Him, how can we truly operate in love? We know Him through the study of His Word as recorded in the holy Scriptures, the Bible. Most people have heard the Scripture verse which says: **"God so loved the world, that he gave his only begotten Son."** (John 3:16) This is the kind of love God expects us to show our spouses. You will not find it where many people look for it. It's not on TV, nor in the best-seller novel, nor in a prostitute's arms, nor in most churches. It can only be truly found in the Word of God. God's love is giving . . . it is bearing hurt . . . it is obedience . . . it is commitment . . . it is forgiving . . . **"70 times seven;"** it is what keeps marriage going when natural love falters or dies. **"Then came Peter to him, and said, Lord, how oft shall my brother sin against me, and I forgive him? till seven times? Jesus saith unto him, I say not unto thee, Until seven times: but, Until seventy times seven."** (Matt. 18:21) **"But if ye forgive not men their trespasses, neither will your Father forgive your trespasses."** (Matt. 6:15) Both love and forgiveness are acts of your free will that God gives to you to control in obedience or disobedience to His Word. You choose to love or not to love. Both love and forgiveness are **active** aspects of an on-going Biblical love.

There are five different types of love that may be a part of a successful marriage: that characterized by physical sexual desire; that characterized by romance; that characterized by family loyalty; that characterized by friendship; that characterized by total commitment. This latter love is called agape. Very few people ever give or receive this type of love for it knows no limits. It continues no matter how much a mate may dislike his/her spouse's behavior. Unconditional love means that a spouse will go out looking for a mate even when that mate has run away to become a prostitute. This kind of love does not compute in society's eyes. The world tells us that agape love is not normal - and it's not. It is, however, what God expects if you are faced with a situation which demands agape love. It is what was mentioned above regarding God's definition of love: it is giving, bearing hurt, obedience, forgiving - total commitment.

A visible symbol of this continuing love is the wedding ring. "The wedding ring is the outward and visible sign of an inward and spiritual <u>bond</u>. It is one unbroken circle to symbolize unending love, visible evidence of this covenant agreement that you have entered into." [6] (See page 32.) An entire book in the Old Testament has been devoted to such an example of unending agape love, Hosea. Hosea's wife became a prostitute. This prophet was commanded of God to go and get his wife, to bring her back home, and to love her **"according to the love of the Lord . . . "** (Hosea 3:3)

An even more incredible example of agape love has been given for man to study and duplicate in the New Testament. Here is an entire book devoted to one man's <u>love</u> for murderers, thieves, liars, homosexuals, adulterers, fornicators, alcoholics - all who sin. Jesus Christ, Himself, volunteered to be nailed to a cross and suffer the ultimate in humiliation and rejection to show this agape love for all mankind. He only asks that man turn away from sin and to Him. This He calls **repentance**. Repentance is not stopping sin because you were caught. It means that you turn from that sin because your heart is changed, that the trespass is something abhorred. The repentant person is grieved to his inner soul and wants to have nothing to do with that which is an abomination to God: **"Now I rejoice, not that ye were made sorry, but that ye sorrowed to repentance . . . For <u>godly sorrow</u> worketh repentance to salvation not to be repented of: but the sorrow of the world worketh death."** (II Cor. 7:9,10)

Agape love, forgiveness, and repentance "to salvation" are accessed through a relationship with the Lord. In our natural strength we fall short of being able to continue in agape love, or to forgive 70 times seven, or to turn from sin which has a strong hold on us. We must follow the Scripture which commands: **"seek ye first the kingdom of God, and his righteousness; and all these things shall be added unto you."** (Matt. 6:33)

Was Christ foolish to willingly be nailed to a cross so that man would have a provision to be forgiven for his repented of sins - a blood sacrifice? Is it foolish today for a mate to love his/her spouse as commanded by God . . . until death physically separates them? Succinctly summarized in the last statement of the marriage ceremony, on page 33, is the truth and consequences of the marriage-covenant: **"so live together in this life that in the world to come you may have life everlasting."**[8]

The Order for the Solemnization of Matrimony

Dearly beloved, we are gathered together here in the sight of God and in the presence of these witnesses, to join this man and this woman in holy matrimony; which is an honorable estate, **instituted by God**, and signifying unto us **the <u>mystical</u> <u>union</u>, which exists between Christ and His Church**. It is therefore not to be entered into unadvisedly, but reverently, discreetly, and in the fear of God. Into this holy estate these two persons come now to be joined.

(Speaking to the persons to be married, the Minister shall say:)

I charge you both, as you stand in the <u>presence of God</u>, to remember that <u>**love**</u> and <u>loyalty</u> alone will avail as the foundation of a happy home. If the solemn <u>vows</u> which you are about to make be kept inviolate and if steadfastly you endeavor to do the will of your Heavenly Father, your life will be full of joy, and the home which you are establishing will abide in peace. No other human ties are more tender, no other vows more sacred than those you now assume.

(Then shall the Minister say to the Man:)

_____, wilt thou have this woman to be thy wedded wife, to live together in the holy estate of matrimony? Wilt thou <u>**love**</u> her, comfort her, honor and keep her, in sickness and in health; and forsaking <u>all</u> others, keep thee only unto her, <u>**so long as ye both shall live**</u>?

(The Man shall answer:)

I will.

(Then shall the Minister say to the Woman:)

_____, wilt thou have this man to be thy wedded husband, to live together in the holy estate of matrimony? Wilt thou <u>**love**</u> him, comfort him, honor and keep him, in sickness and in health; and forsaking <u>all</u> others, keep thee only unto him, <u>**so long as ye both shall live**</u>?

(The Woman shall answer:)

I will.

(Then may the Minister say:)

Who giveth this woman to be married to this man?

(The Father of the Woman, or whoever gives her in marriage, shall answer:)

I do.

(Then the Minister, receiving the hand of the Woman from her Father or other Sponsor, shall cause the Man with his right hand to take the Woman by her right hand, and say after him:)

I,_____, take thee,_____, to be my wedded wife, to have and to hold, **from this day forward,**$_4$ **for better, for worse, for richer, for poorer, in sickness and in health, to love and to cherish,**$_5$ **till death us do part,**$_4$ according to **God's holy ordinance**$_1$; and thereto I plight thee my faithfulness.

(Then shall they loose their hands; and the Woman, with her right hand taking the Man by his right hand, shall likewise say after the Minister:)

I,_____, take thee,_____, to be my wedded husband, to have and to hold, **from this day forward,**$_4$ **for better, for worse, for richer, for poorer, in sickness and in health,**$_5$ **to love and to cherish, till death us do part,**$_4$ according to **God's holy ordinance**$_1$; and thereto I plight thee my faithfulness.

(Then shall they loose their hands; and the Man shall give to the Woman a ring, in this manner: the Minister, taking the ring, shall say:)

The wedding ring is the outward and visible sign of an **inward and spiritual bond.** It is one unbroken circle to symbolize **unending love,** visible evidence of this **covenant**$_3$ agreement that you have entered into$_6$.

(The Minister shall then deliver$_6$ the ring to the Man.)

Take it and place it on the third finger of her left hand, and, holding it there, answer the following: Do you,_____, give this ring in promise before God and these witnesses that you will keep this **covenant,**$_3$ and perform these vows? If you agree, say, "I do."

(The Man shall answer:)

I do.

(In case of a double ring ceremony, the Minister shall deliver the other ring to the Woman to put upon the third finger of the Man's left hand, and the Woman, holding the ring there, shall say after the Minister:)

Take it and place it on the third finger of his left hand, and, holding it there, answer the following: Do you,_____, give this ring in promise before God and these witnesses that you will keep this **covenant,**$_3$ and perform these vows? If you agree, say, "I do."

(Then the Woman shall answer:)

I do.

(Then shall the Minister say:)

Let us pray.

O Eternal God, Creator and Preserver of all mankind, Giver of all spiritual grace, the Author of everlasting life; send Thy blessing upon this man and this woman, whom we bless in Thy Name; that they may surely perform and keep the **covenant**$_3$ and **vows** now made <u>between</u> **them and Thee**.

Look graciously upon them, that they may <u>**love,**</u>$_7$ honor, and cherish each other, and so live together in faithfulness and patience, and wisdom and true godliness, that their home may be a haven of blessing and a place of peace: through Jesus Christ our Lord. Amen.

(Then shall the Minister join their right hands together and with his hand on their united hands shall say:)

Forasmuch as _____, and _____, have consented together in holy wedlock, and have witnessed the same before God and this company, and thereto have pledged their faith each to the other, and have declared the same by joining hands, and by giving and receiving rings; I pronounce that they are husband and wife together, in the Name of the Father, and of the Son, and of the Holy Spirit. **What God hath joined together, let not man put asunder**$_8$. Amen.

(Then shall the Minister add this blessing:)

God the Father, the Son, and the Holy Spirit, bless, preserve, and keep you; the Lord mercifully with His favor look upon you; and so fill you with all spiritual blessing and love that you may so **live together in this life that in the world to come you may have** <u>**life everlasting**</u>$_8$. Amen.

CHAPTER 3
WHY DIDN'T JOSEPH HAVE MARY STONED TO DEATH?

For those who have not studied Jewish customs and regulations as recorded in the Old Testament, this question may seem to be a puzzling, almost sacrilegious query. It is, however, based upon an important teaching surrounding the birth of Jesus Christ. Recall that in Chapter One Adam and Eve chose to disobey what they had been warned would bring death to them. One of the positive outcomes of this rebellion was the first of over some 300 prophecies regarding the explicit time, place, and circumstances of the miraculous birth of Christ: **"and I will put enmity between thee and the woman, and between thy seed and her seed."** (Gen. 3:15) This was thousands of years before the event actually came to pass, and tells us that this conception would be different from any other in that the Savior would be born of (through) a seed of (through) a woman rather than the normal biological conception by man which requires that the sperm be transmitted by the male. (One-half of the genetic instructions comes from the male sperm; the blood of woman and the fetus do not mix.) Even more miraculous is the fact that some 700 to 800 years before this birth, man is clearly told that Christ will be born of a virgin: **"Behold a virgin shall conceive, and bear a son."** (Isa. 7:14) (Along with the time, place, and many other minute details of Christ's life through Old Testament prophecy, we have been also foretold that Christ would be born through the lineage of the house of King David.)

Adam, when he was born, had perfect blood, but when he sinned, it was corrupted not only for himself, but for all of mankind. Jesus, on the other hand, had pure, undefiled blood, because **"that which is conceived in her is of the**

Holy Ghost" . . . through a virgin. (Matt 1:20) Thus, the blood that Jesus received via the Holy Ghost caused him to have <u>incorruptible</u>, pure blood. He took on the likeness of man in a physical body but not man's sin nature. Throughout the New Testament, we find a constant contrast noted between the corruptible blood of man and the incorruptible or innocent blood of Jesus. For example, Judas remarked, as recorded in Matthew 27:4: **"I have sinned in that I have betrayed innocent blood."**

It was mentioned above that prophesy also foretold that Christ's parents would be of royal bloodline - descendants of King David. The Jewish nation knew this well. This is why we have in the book of Matthew a somewhat different viewpoint of this revelation of the Messiah's birth than we do in Luke. Matthew was written for all of mankind but especially to answer questions for the Jewish Christians to prove that Jesus was indeed the promised Messiah as well as other issues relating to their customs. The Gentiles did not look for specific proof of lineage nor did they practice many of the Jewish customs, especially those relating to engagement and punishment for sexual sin. Thus we find a different emphasis in the remaining three books of the Gospels, Mark, Luke, and John. Intricately interwoven within the Matthew account of Christ's conception and birth is an explanation of the Jewish customs regarding the betrothal (engagement) period. As a part of this is the Mosaic custom of stoning those caught in adultery. Without an understanding of Old Testament Jewish customs, most readers would misinterpret the important underlying messages taught in the book of Matthew.

What were the supernatural circumstances surrounding the birth of Christ?

Comparing and contrasting the account of the birth of Christ in Matthew and in Luke, we find that in only Matthew does the author detail the genealogy of Jesus. Christ was born of a virgin not only because His birth was to be supernatural and extraordinary, but also because it was to be spotless and pure and without any stain of sin. The "seed" of Mary was conceived by the Holy Ghost: **"for that which is conceived in her is of the Holy Ghost."** (Matt. 1:20)

Because of Old Testament prophecies, it had to be proven to the Jewish Christians that Jesus was a son of David and a son of Abraham. The Jews were very exact in preserving these records. Thus in Matthew, Chapter One, we read what appears to be a boring account of "begats." This, however, was important to prove: **"the generation of Jesus Christ the son of David, the son of Abraham"** through 14 generations down through and including Joseph. These people always kept their genealogies by the males, but we know that Mary was of the same tribe and family as was Joseph, so that both by His mother and by His adopted earthly father, Jesus was born of the house of David. **"And Jacob begat Joseph the husband of Mary, of whom was born Jesus, who is called Christ."** (Matt. 1:16) In Luke, the Scriptures only mention the house of David with no genealogy: **"To a virgin espoused to a man whose name was Joseph, of the house of David; and the virgin's name was Mary."** (Luke 1:27)

The next point of emphasis is that Mary was a virgin, not only in the foretelling from Isaiah and other Old Testament books but also in the book of Luke. (See above.) To further lay important background, we must study another important fact. Joseph and Mary were engaged, not married, when the angel, Gabriel, came to each of them regarding what was to come to pass. Mary was **"espoused to a man whose name was Joseph."** Notice a slight difference in the account specifically designed to minister to the Jews rather than the Gentiles as in Luke. In Matthew, we find not only the account of the engagement, but the fact that Jewish custom during the betrothal period required that even though they were not married, they were called husband and wife. This is recorded only in the account in Matthew: **"Now the birth of Jesus Christ was on this wise: When as his mother Mary was espoused to Joseph, before they came together, she was found with child of the Holy Ghost. Then Joseph her husband, being a just man, and not willing to make her a public example, was minded to put her away privily. But while he thought on these things, behold, the angel of the Lord** appeared unto him in a dream, saying, Joseph, thou son of David, fear not to take unto thee Mary <u>thy wife</u>: for that which is conceived in her is of the Holy Ghost. And she shall bring forth a son, and thou shalt call his name Jesus: for he shall save his people from their sins . . . Then Joseph being raised from sleep did as the angel of the Lord had bidden him, and <u>took unto him</u> his wife: And <u>knew her not</u> till she had brought forth her firstborn son." (Matt. 1:18-25) (Recall from the teaching in Chapter Two that the act of sex is not a part of the marriage-covenant but a privilege of marriage. Here we are told that it was at this time that Joseph and Mary were united in God's sight, but there was no sexual union between them until after the birth of Christ.)

In Luke, we have quite a different emphasis. We have the feelings, the fears, perhaps that any female virgin might ponder: **"Then said Mary unto the angel, How shall this be, seeing** <u>I know not a man</u>? Perhaps she thought: "What will my mom and dad say? They've been so careful throughout my childhood to protect me so that I might remain a virgin until marriage. What a shameful thing to have one's chastity taken before this time. And what will the leaders in the synagogue say? How can I go worship in the temple if they find out that I'm pregnant without a husband? What will my friends say when I walk in and try to explain that I am pregnant? What about the ridicule from people even after the birth of this child?" Remember that Jesus was indeed accused of being conceived through an act of fornication not long before his crucifixion: **"Then said they to him, we be not born of <u>fornication</u>."** (John 8:41) "And Joseph, oh my, what will he do? Will he have me stoned to death, according to Mosaic law, for what he thinks is fornication?"

We could perhaps imagine some of Joseph's perplexity: "Not Mary; how could she? She's always been so faithful. She has been a woman of prayer and obedience." We find recorded from Joseph's reaction that he loved Mary so much that instead of doing what the Old Testament law allowed, **"being a just man, and not willing to make her a public example, was minded to put her away privily."** (Matt.

1:19) He would not proceed to marry her, but decided "to put her away" (<u>divorce</u> this one to whom he was <u>engaged</u>) but as privately as possible. This tells of Joseph's tender affection for Mary. "But wait a minute," you say. "What is this reference to killing Mary by having her stoned to death?" By the Mosaic law, a **betrothed virgin**, if she played the harlot, was to be stoned to death: **"If a damsel that is a virgin be <u>betrothed</u> unto a <u>husband</u>, and a man find her in the city, and lie with her; Then ye shall bring them both out unto the gate of that city, and ye shall stone them with stones that they die; the damsel because she cried not, being in the city; and the man, because he hath humbled his neighbor's <u>wife</u>: so thou shalt put away evil from among you."** (Deu. 22:23,24) Note, that there was a distinction between those partaking in fornication (not married) and those partaking in adultery (married): **"If a man be found lying with a woman <u>married to a husband</u>, then they shall both of them die, both the man that lay with the woman, and the woman: <u>so shalt thou put away evil</u> from Israel."** (Deu. 22:22)

So then, if one were to follow the Mosaic Law, there would be no question regarding what many call "the exception clause." Those who were involved in either fornication or adultery were put to death. Why? The answer was so that <u>evil</u>, adultery and fornication, would be blotted out. If man, today, followed this teaching, thousands would be put to death every day either by stoning or by other means!

Joseph, here, as Jesus directs in the New Testament, either forgave what he thought was fornication or was immediately convinced that the case was not so against his beloved Mary. The angel did remind Joseph of his lineage to David, perhaps that he might be prepared to receive this "news" about his betrothed as everyone knew that the Messiah was to be a descendant from David. **"Joseph, <u>thou son of David</u>, fear not to take unto thee Mary <u>thy wife</u>."** (Matt. 1:20)

What does the Bible say about second marriages?

We have, through a study of the Scriptures, seen two

differing principles between the Old and New Testaments regarding sexual sin. In the Old Testament, fornication and adultery were immediately punishable by death. In the New Testament teachings, we are commanded to forgive and turn from this behavior else it eventually end up in eternal death. These "customs" of the Old Testament times, we do not live by. They were set in place to control the sins of man during Moses' day. Man, today "plays" with some of the Old Testament customs. For example, some will say that once a couple obtains a divorce, neither can go back to the original mate, quoting Deuteronomy 24:4: **"Her former husband, which sent her away may not take her again to be his wife."** The purpose for this prohibition was to prevent a wicked practice which the Egyptians had of changing wives. We know that in the New Testament, man is told never to change wives while a one-flesh spouse is still living because it is adultery in God's eyes. **"For the woman which hath a husband is bound by the law to her husband so long as he liveth . . . So then if, while her husband liveth, she be married to another man, she shall be called an adulteress."** (Rom. 7:2,3) Additionally, let's look at the practice of misapplying Old Testament regulations to excuse sin in the Twentieth century. If we are to say that Deuteronomy 24:4 is applicable today, then should not other regulations of that day be followed today? Let's look at four of these, none of which does man try to say applies today:

1. **"And the man that committeth adultery with another man's wife, even he that committeth adultery with his neighbor's wife, the adulterer and the adulteress shall surely be put to death."** (Lev. 20:10)
2. **"When a man hath taken a new wife, he shall not go out to war, neither shall he be charged with any business: but he shall be free at home one year."** (Deu. 24:5)
3. **". . . neither shall a garment mingled of linen and woollen come upon thee."** (Lev. 19:19) (This prohibition might mean that we would be sinning if we wore clothing made of more than one fiber!)

4. "And this shall be a statute for ever unto you: that in the seventh month, on the tenth day of the month, ye shall afflict your souls, and do no work at all." (Lev. 16:29)

If we study even just the first five books of the Old Testament, we would find hundreds of prohibitions, customs, and regulations which we do not follow today. Many of these were put in place to deal with the rebellious nature of man. One such example was the "bill of divorcement" which Moses gave so that it would be clear that the wife was not being divorced for adultery or fornication, and thus avoid death. Man today, as when Jesus ministered here, tries to "use" this "regulatory practice" as a scapegoat to excuse sin: **"And the Pharisees came to him, and asked him," (Jesus) "is it lawful for a man to put away his wife? tempting him. And he answered and said unto them, What did Moses command you? And they said, Moses suffered to write a bill of divorcement, and to put her away. And Jesus answered and said unto them, For the hardness of your heart he wrote you this precept. But from the beginning of the creation God made them male and female . . . What therefore God hath joined together, let not man put asunder."** (Mark 10:2-9) Here and in Matthew 19, we have the same incident, but note that following the initial same setup where the Pharisees came to Jesus **tempting Him,** and Jesus tells them that Moses allowed the "bill of divorcement" for hardness of heart (not for adultery), we have an important variation between the two accounts. The first, in Matthew, which we learned above was written to the Jews, has an exception for the fornication discussed regarding Mary and Joseph in Matthew 1:18-25. The Jews had a custom which the Gentiles did not; that being, if a damsel or single woman were caught in fornication, she would be stoned to death. But, a Jewish betrothed man, who was just such as Joseph would "put her away privily"; that is, he would divorce her privately. A divorce during the betrothal period was allowed.

Matthew 19:9 says: **"And I" (Jesus) "say unto you, whosoever shall put away his wife, except it be for fornication, and shall marry another, committeth adultery: and whoso marrieth her which is put away doth commit**

adultery." So they could "put away" or divorce a "wife" to whom they were engaged to be married, because of fornication. If they "put away" a wife to whom they were married, and married someone else, this was and still is adultery. In Mark 10:11-12, written to the Gentiles, the Jewish exception to deal with fornication during the betrothal period is not mentioned. Jesus just says unto them: "**Whosoever shall put away his wife, and marry another, committeth adultery against her. And if a woman shall put away her husband, and be married to another, she committeth adultery.**" In Matthew 19:10, the disciples very much understood the seriousness of what Jesus had said. The disciples replied: "**If the case of the man be so with his wife, it is not good to marry.**"

An "exception clause" for adultery is not in the Bible, but it has been so frequently misquoted as Scripture that many believe it is there and will often even look at the "**except it be for fornication**" and read it as being "except it be for adultery." Many of the people who misuse the phrase, "**except it be for fornication**" are the ones who are looking for a "Biblical excuse" for marrying a second spouse but ironically are often the very ones who have been involved in the sin of adultery. We also find those who say that the spouse sinned against is the "innocent" party and thus is free to marry someone else. Again, this is not Biblical. As was shown in Chapter Two, nothing other than death breaks the marriage-covenant. If adultery were a "Biblical excuse" for divorce, then a woman/man could merely accuse his/her spouse of looking at another person with lust and thereby be given a "Scriptural divorce": "**But I say unto you, that whosoever looketh on a woman to lust after her hath committed adultery with her already in his heart.**" (Matt. 5:28)

This same exception for fornication is repeated one other time - again in Matthew, but in this instance, a real emphasis is placed upon one of the ramifications resulting from the initial sin of divorcing one's mate. The mate not initiating a divorce in most instances because of loneliness, hurt, financial or peer and family pressure, lust, ignorance or rebellion to the Word, subsequently also marries another spouse. S/he does not obey the specific <u>command</u> of the Lord: **"But, and if she depart, let her remain unmarried, <u>or</u> be reconciled to her husband: and let not the husband put away his wife."** (I Cor. 7:10-11) The once "innocent" spouse proceeds to put him-herself into a state of adultery. S/he is in essence also "putting away" a one-flesh mate but doesn't need to "sanction" illicit behavior with a civil lawsuit as society does not agree with the definition of adultery as given in the Bible nor does it believe that marriage is "from this day forward . . . till death us do part."

Look at Matthew 5:31,32: "**<u>It hath been said,</u>** (Notice, Jesus specifically says <u>it</u> not <u>I</u> have said.) **Whosoever shall put away his wife, let him give her a writing of divorcement: <u>But I say unto you,</u> That whosoever shall put away his wife, <u>saving for the cause of fornication,</u> causeth her to commit adultery: and whosoever shall marry her that is divorced committeth adultery.**" So then, if we remove the exception for "divorcing" during the betrothal period, we have: "**But I say unto you, That whosoever shall put away his wife <u>causeth</u> her to commit adultery: and whosoever shall marry her that is divorced committeth adultery.**" Four additional things seem apparent here:

1. As in Matthew 19 and Mark 10, Jesus does not take credit for the "exception clause," "**It hath been said . . .**"
2. Sin is far reaching. It never affects only the person initiating it. That person <u>causes</u> others to also sin by way of consent or being a catalyst to others to "follow suit."
3. Even though a person may have been what society calls the "innocent person," just as with Adam and Eve, when Eve said that the serpent caused her to sin, she was still held responsible for what she did. Consequently, here in this Scripture portion, Jesus says everyone involved becomes an adulterer or adulteress . . . "**and <u>whosoever</u> shall marry her that is divorced committeth adultery.**"
4. If we cause others to sin, we will be held

responsible not only for our own sin, but for leading others astray: **"Whosoever therefore shall break one of these least commandments, and shall teach men so . . . ye shall in no case enter into the kingdom of heaven."** (Matt. 5:19,20) Solomon, called the wisest man of Old Testament times, said: **"Whoso causeth the righteous to go astray in an evil way, he shall fall himself into his own pit."** (Pro. 28:10) Malachi, the prophet warned **". . . ye have caused many to stumble at the law; the Lord will cut off the man that doeth this."** (Mal. 2:8,12)

What is repentance?

Some will say, "but that makes divorce an unforgivable sin and God says that only blasphemy of the Holy Ghost is the unforgivable sin." No, divorce is not an unforgivable sin. All sin, except that just mentioned, can be forgiven but . . . sin is only forgiven if we repent. This means that we are sorry for it, abhor it, and we stop doing what God calls sin. Godly repentance means that there is such sorrow as shall cause a complete change of action. Judas, for example, repented of his sin against our Lord (Matt. 27:3-8) but he did not change his lifestyle. Paul, the apostle, in II Corinthians 7:9,10 contrasts the repentance of the world, which says, "I'm sorry," but continues in sin, with that which God calls true repentance: **"Now I rejoice, not that ye were made sorry, but that ye sorrowed to repentance: for ye were made sorry after a godly manner, that ye might receive damage by us in nothing. For godly sorrow worketh repentance to salvation not to be repented of: but the sorrow of the world worketh death."** True repentance is impossible without acting upon what the Word says. Just believing is not enough. We must **do** what the apostle James said: **"the devils also believe, and tremble. But wilt thou know, O vain man, that faith without works is dead?"** (Jas. 2:19,20) When we repent, we turn from that sin and do not return to it; that is, we don't repent of our repentance by returning to the practice of a former transgression.

If someone is practicing a lifestyle that God says is sin, he is lost - according to the Scriptures, no matter how much he says that he is sorry for it. Review again the list of actions which God says is sin. These "lost" people are fornicators, idolaters, adulterers, effeminate, abusers of themselves with mankind (homosexuals), thieves, drunkards. (I Cor. 6:9,10) None of these sins is unforgivable _if_ the person committing that sin hates it enough to run from it - to have absolutely nothing to do with it again. Let's imagine we have set up a series of interviews with some of the above-described people.

THIEF

Picture a conversation with a "professional" thief. He* has come to you and wants to know what he must do to be saved. You would probably say to him: "You must accept Jesus Christ as your Lord and Savior which means that you must live according to what the Word says. You may no longer have as your profession, stealing." "But," says he, "this is how I make a living. It was never considered wrong in my household. My father/mother died a very rich, happy person by stealing from others." "No," you say, "'**Be not deceived . . . thieves . . . shall not inherit the kingdom of God.**' The true evidence that you have repented will be when you agree with what God says by obeying the Word: '**He that saith, I know him, and keepeth not his commandments, is a liar, and the truth is not in him.**'" (I John 2:4)

FORNICATOR/PROSTITUTE

Picture a conversation with a "professional" fornicator/ prostitute. He has come to you and wants to know what he must do to be saved. You would probably say to

---

*The pronoun he is used through the mock interviews, but the message refers to both male and female. The Scriptures likewise are written assuming the reader knows that commands apply to both male and female.

him: "You must accept Jesus Christ as your Lord and Savior which means that you must live according to what the Word says. You may no longer have as your profession, prostitution." "But," he says, "this is how I make a living. It was never considered wrong in my household. My mother/father died a very rich, happy person living in this lifestyle." "No," you say, "'**Be not deceived . . . fornicators . . . shall not inherit the kingdom of God.**' You must stop doing what God considers sin. Biblically consistent evidence that you've been born into God's family will be when you agree with God and stop doing what He considers sin."

HOMOSEXUAL

Picture a conversation with a "professional" sodomite, or homosexual, the former being the Biblical term for a person practicing this lifestyle. He has come to you and wants to know what he must do to be saved. You would probably say to him: "You must accept Jesus Christ as your Lord and Savior which means that you must live according to what the Word says. You may no longer have as your profession, homosexuality." "But," he says, "this is how I make a living. It was never considered wrong in my household. My father/mother died a very rich, happy person by living as a homosexual." "No," you say, "'**Be not deceived . . . effeminate or abusers of themselves with mankind . . . shall not inherit the kingdom of God.**' Biblically consistent evidence that you have been born into God's family will be when you agree with God and stop doing what He considers sin."

ADULTERER

Picture a conversation with a "professional" adulterer. He has come to you and wants to know what he must do to be saved. Would you say, "in Truth," to him: "You must accept Jesus Christ as your Lord and Savior which means that you must live according to what the Word says. You may no longer have as your lifestyle, adultery"? "But," he says, "this is how I make a living. It was never considered wrong in my household. My father/mother died a very rich, happy person while living as a adulterer." "No," you say, '**Be not deceived . . . adulterers . . . shall not inherit**

the kingdom of God.' True Biblical evidence that you have repented will be when you agree with what God says and stop doing what He considers sin. **'He that saith, I know him, and keepeth not his commandments, is a liar, and the truth is not in him.'"** (I John 2:4)

Some will still go back to unscriptural thinking and continue to respond: "Is divorce the only sin that God will not forgive?" No, but remember, the real question concerns <u>what it is that you are asking God to forgive</u>. A one-flesh marriage is not sin. The <u>sin</u> is unforgiveness toward a one-flesh mate and/or a second marriage which God calls adultery. These are the trespasses from which a person must repent. Why is it that we have no trouble telling the thief, the murderer, the homosexual, or the alcoholic that they must stop doing what God considers sin in order to inherit the Kingdom of God but that only adulterers can continue sinning and God will look the other way? This seems to be especially true by people "in the church" who feel that God's commandment, **"Thou shalt not commit adultery,"** (Rom. 14:9) applies only to those who do not attend church!

Be not deceived, **"God is no respector of persons."** **"Behold, ye trust in lying words, that cannot profit. Will ye steal, murder, and commit adultery, and swear falsely, and burn incense unto Baal, and walk after other gods whom ye know not; And come and stand before me in this house, which is called by my name, and say, We are delivered to do all these abominations?"** (Jer. 7:8-10)

CHAPTER 4
WHAT DID JESUS REALLY SAY TO THE WOMAN AT THE WELL?

There is a story so often repeated by Christians and non-Christians, television and radio evangelists, as well as ministers that we need to study - the woman at the well and the woman caught in adultery. Why? Because principles from two <u>differing</u> accounts between the Lord and people involved in adultery have been incorrectly combined and Biblical principles misapplied. We are warned in the second chapter of II Peter: **"But there were false prophets also among the people, even as <u>there shall be among you</u>, who privily shall bring in damnable heresies, even denying the Lord that bought them, and bring upon themselves swift destruction. And many shall follow their pernicious ways."**

Like so many Scriptures regarding the sanctity of marriage, man repeats what he hears over and over and will be convinced that it is Biblical Truth because it "seems to make sense," and because the person verbalizing it sounds authoritative. It is important to learn a command of the Lord. **Each of us** must search the Scriptures so that we will not be deceived into following false teachers and their teachings. **"Study to show <u>thyself</u> approved unto God, a workman that needeth not to be ashamed, <u>rightly dividing</u> the word of truth,"** " **. . . beware lest ye also, being led away with the error of the wicked, fall from your own steadfastness."** (II Tim. 2:15; II Peter 3:17) **"For my thoughts are not your thoughts, neither are your ways my ways, saith the Lord." "For I am the Lord, I change not." "Jesus Christ the same yesterday, and today, and for ever"; "for ever, O Lord, thy word is settled in heaven."** (Isa. 57:8; Mal. 3:6; Heb. 13:8; Psa. 119:89)

Satan is a "scholar" of the Scriptures; man rarely is.

As with Adam and Eve in the beginning, **slightly** altering God's Word changed all of history, including man's relationship with God, the tilling of the earth, and the deceitfulness of the heart. Eve said, **"But of the fruit of the tree which is in the midst of the garden, God hath said, Ye shall not eat of it, neither shall ye touch it, lest ye die."** (Gen. 3:3) As man might typically believe his lustful desires to be harmless Satan injects, **"And the serpent said unto the woman, Ye shall not surely die."** He adds what sounds right, "postscript rationale." **"For God doth know that in the day ye eat thereof, then your eyes shall be opened, and ye shall be as gods, knowing good and evil.*** The "unseen danger" behind all of this deception is that once man finds someone to approve of behavior he knows to be wrong, the heart-hardening process sets in: **"because they received not the love of the truth, that they might be saved. And for this cause God shall send them strong delusion, that they should believe a lie: That they all might be damned who believed not the truth, but had pleasure in unrighteousness."** (II Thess. 2:10-12.) Man, in his delusion of "getting away" with sin, does not know that this is part of God's judgment - **"Speaking lies in hypocrisy; having their conscience seared."** (I Tim. 4:2) "

Notice Eve's reaction after the serpent's "postscript rationale," and compare it with Genesis 3:3 before she had affirmation from someone whose intent it is to manipulate man into rebelling against the Truth of the Word of God. **"And when the woman saw that the tree was good for food, and that it was pleasant to the eyes, and a tree to be desired to make one wise, she took of the fruit thereof, and did eat, and gave also unto her husband with her: and he did eat."**

With the above forewarning and review of the principles involved in the "fall" of Adam and Eve, follow along with your Bible as we listen in on the conversation between Jesus

---

*This is a tenet promoted today by the religion of secular humanism. (See page 144.)

and the woman at the well. "**Jesus answered and said unto her, whosoever drinketh of the water shall thirst again: But <u>whosoever</u> drinketh of the water that I shall give shall never thirst; but the water that I shall give him shall be in him a well of water springing up into everlasting life. The woman saith unto him, Sir, give me this water, that I thirst not, neither come hither to draw. Jesus saith unto her, Go call thy husband, and come hither. The woman answered and said, <u>I have no husband</u>. Jesus said unto her, Thou hast well said, <u>I have no husband: For thou hast had five husbands; and he whom thou now hast is not thy husband: in that saidst thou truly</u>.**" (John 4:13-18)

The following account is how man explains the scene of the woman at the well to others. He uses "postscript rationale," which sounds correct, and it is - <u>partially</u>:

> "You can't fool God. He's well aware of her past and she's trying to evade the issue . . . and He convicts her. In Judea, her behavior would be a <u>capital</u> crime. She's an adulteress (but here, the speaker twists the word "slightly"). Jesus further replies <u>to this woman with **five** husbands, I do not condemn thee. Let the one who is without sin cast the first stone</u>. Thus, we see <u>grace</u> here. The convercation goes on and we see her accusers all leave as they were not without sin."

Notice that this latter "postscript rationale" is not in John Four. As we will discover, it is from John Eight and a different set of circumstances, time, place, and people. Nowhere in His discourse with the woman caught in adultery (John Eight), does Jesus imply that this woman had five husbands.

This twisting of the Word is used to excuse people in adulterous marriage relationships. What man today "caught in adultery" wants to hear is that the woman at the well had <u>five</u> husbands, and God forgave her <u>and</u> said that she could remain with whichever husband she was presently living with; incorrectly interpolating that if the Lord "finds you" while you are in a second, third, fourth, or fifth marriage, you can remain in that marriage. "Thus we see **grace*** here!" Man incorrectly says God will condone what He calls sin and tell the transgressor - just don't do it again. No, God requires repentance . . . **"Shall we continue in sin, that grace may abound? God forbid."** If a person's heart has not been hardened against the Word of God, s/he will "hear" and turn from sin; otherwise, rebellion will continue as only **"My sheep hear my voice, and I know them, and they follow me."** (John 10:27) (In the Greek, this statement is in the present indicative which would be "keep on hearing" or "are in the habit of hearing and obeying.")

Let's look at the Scriptures that deal with Jesus extending **grace** to a woman caught in the act of adultery. In John Eight we find the following account: **"Jesus went unto the mount of Olives. And early in the morning he came again into the temple, and all the people came unto him;**

---

* Grace is a word so much abused by those looking to justify sin. They misuse the Biblical meaning of grace when they say that God shows love by excusing disobedience. This is heresy. Grace is tied to obedience as is God's definition of love: **"But whoso keepeth his word, in him verily is the love of God perfected: hereby know we that we are in him. And hereby we do know that we know him, if we keep his commandments. He that saith, I know him, and keepeth not his commandments, is a liar,** and the truth is not in him." (I John 3:3-5) **"Thou shalt not commit adultery, Thou shalt not kill, Thou shalt not steal, Thou shalt not bear false witness, Thou shalt not covet."** (Rom. 13:9) Paul, in another discourse, reinforces the "Biblical intent" of grace: **"What shall we say then? Shall we continue in sin, that grace may abound? God forbid. How shall we, that are dead to sin, live any longer therein?"** (Rom. 6:1,2) In Titus, we are told that it is the grace of God that brings salvation by teaching us that being saved demands **"denying ungodliness and worldly lusts. We should live soberly, righteously, and godly in this present world."** (Titus 3:11,12) and he sat down, and taught them. And the scribes and Pharisees brought unto him a woman taken in adultery; and when they had set her in the midst, They say unto him, Master, this woman was taken in adultery, in the very act. Now <u>Moses</u> in the law <u>commanded</u> us, that <u>such should be stoned</u>: but what sayest thou? This they said, <u>tempting him</u>, that they might have to accuse him. But Jesus stooped down, and with his finger wrote on the ground, as though he heard them not. So when they continued asking him, he lifted up himself, and said unto them, He that is without sin among you, let him first cast a stone at her. And again he stooped down, and wrote on the ground. And they which heard it, <u>being convicted</u> by their own conscience, went out one by one, beginning at the eldest, even unto the last: and Jesus was left alone, and the woman standing in the midst. When Jesus had lifted up himself, and saw none but the woman, he said unto her, Woman, where are those thine accusers? hath no man condemned thee? She said, No man, Lord. And Jesus said unto her, Neither do I condemn thee: go, and sin no more."

What was Jesus' message to the woman at the well?

It's important to take an in-depth look at each of these two accounts. First, the woman <u>with five husbands</u> takes us to a city in Samaria called Sychar as recorded in John 4:4. There was a great deal of hostility between the Jews and Samaritans. These two peoples were such malicious enemies that Christ had earlier told his disciples: "**go not . . . into any city of the Samaritans enter ye not.**" (Matt. 10:5) Yet, by "Divine Providence," this Samaritan woman either fortuitously or Providentially has an encounter with the Lord which He chooses to record permanently for man to study. There must be something quite significant here for our creator to inscribe for posterity this confrontation but leave buried in silence such discourses as those with Moses and Elias on the mount!

The stage is set. The woman at the well and Christ banter concerning the living water (eternal life) available through Christ as opposed to the water drawn from a man-made well. He continues by cleverly broaching the subject for which He perhaps had come - to provide "grace" for one headed for eternal death: **"Go, call thy husband, and come hither."** And we read the reply of the woman, **"I have no husband."** To which Jesus said, **"Thou hast well said, I have no husband: For thou <u>hast</u> had five husbands; and he whom thou <u>now</u> <u>hast</u> is not thy husband: in that saidst thou truly.** The woman appears to evade the judgment while at the same time convicting herself when she replied, **"I have no husband."** Being careful to avoid the truth of the matter, her reply intimated that she perhaps was a widow or that she had never been married.

Jesus apparently discussed much more about this woman's intimate life than what is recorded. It had such an impact on her that she **"<u>left her waterpot</u> and went her way into the city, and saith to the men, Come, see a man, <u>which told me things that ever I did</u>"**! (John 4:28,29) Christ, however, chose to leave as a record for us to study that conversation concerning her relationships with five so-called husbands. The severe reproof continues as Jesus responds, **"He <u>whom thou now hast</u> is <u>not</u> <u>thy husband</u>."** She most likely was either never married to this man or in all probability because of the choice of the word "hast," she in accordance with society was living with a "husband" when either he had some other wife, or her former husband(s) were living. In essence, she was living in adultery. What she intended as a denial of the fact (that she had none with whom she lived <u>as a husband</u>) Christ affirmed. In so doing, He turned her intended denial into a self-confession of her sin. The Samaritan woman confirmed Christ's allegation with her response: **"Sir, I perceive that thou art a prophet."** (John 4:19)

What was Jesus' message to the woman caught in adultery?

Now let's move from Sychar, this city of Samaria, to the mount of Olives, some 30 miles south. This is where the narrative about the "woman caught in adultery" occurred. The episode of the "woman at the well" took place just outside Herod's jurisdiction at the time when Herod had imprisoned John the Baptist. Apparent immediately should be the fact that Jesus would not have, in the same conversation, been talking to this Samaritan woman in two different places so distant, the latter an area where the woman at the well would have been most unwelcome.

The Pharisees came to Jesus <u>with the purpose of trying to trap Him</u>. They brought <u>only</u> the woman whom they said was <u>caught in the act of adultery</u>. As we saw in Chapter Three, under Jewish "law" <u>all</u> caught in adultery were to be stoned to death: "**And the scribes and Pharisees brought unto him a woman taken in adultery; and when they had set her in the midst, They say unto him, this woman was taken in adultery, in the very act. Now Moses <u>in the law</u> commanded <u>us</u>, <u>that such should be stoned</u>: <u>but</u> what sayest thou? This they said, tempting him, <u>that they might have to accuse him</u>**." (John 8:3-6) This was not the law of the Gentiles (the Romans), but this ruling government allowed the Jews to continue with their custom of stoning to death adulterers and fornicators. Mosiac "procedural due process" (See page 150.) dictated that those caught in adultery were to be brought before the ecclesiastical court. Jesus was teaching in the temple so the Pharisees rightfully brought the woman to Him. "**Jesus went unto the mount of Olives. And early in the morning he came again into the temple, and all the people came unto him; and he sat down, and taught them. And the scribes and Pharisees brought unto him a woman taken in adultery.**" (John 8:1-3) They quote the Mosaic "statute" under which this adulteress was to be stoned to death. They hoped to trap this teacher who was "legislating" new laws of love and forgiveness while making even stronger applications of the ten commandments: "**But I say unto you, That <u>whosoever</u> <u>looketh</u> on a woman to lust after her hath committed adultery with her already in his heart.**" (Matt. 5:28) (Note that the Lord in most of His commands does not have differing rules for men or women or for the saved or "unsaved." He treats us generically with the pronoun <u>whosoever</u>, to let us know there are no exceptions.)

Instead of debating the Mosaic law with them, Jesus let the accusers apply His teaching to themselves. He wisely answered, "**He that is without sin among you, let him first**

cast a stone at her." Did a barrage of stones begin to be hurled at this adulteress? No, instead each of them turned and left for they, too, had been guilty of some form of adultery or other sin. Justice would have it that the accusers might have been stoned also. Those today who wish to quote part of the Jewish customs such as Deuteronomy 24:4 may need to be reminded that they, too, could possibly come under the Mosaic "statute" to be stoned to death, not only for the actual act but for even looking with lust!

The Scriptures continue: **"And they which heard it, being convicted by their own conscience, went out one by one, beginning at the eldest, even unto the last: and Jesus was left alone, and the woman standing in the midst. When Jesus had lifted up himself, and saw none but the woman, he said unto her, Woman, where are those thine accusers? hath no man condemned thee? She said, No man, Lord. And Jesus said unto her, Neither do I condemn thee: go, and sin no more."** In Jesus' act of **grace**, we see an example of a woman with a heart which apparently was not hardened to the point where there was no room for repentance. With this woman, He was able to attend to the work for which He came into the world; that is, to bring sinners to repentance so that they might be saved. He likewise extended this **grace** unto the prosecutors. They sought to trap Him; His purpose, however, was to **convict** and **convert** them as He does man today. One only has to **turn from sin and to receive** Jesus Christ as Lord and Master to truly receive the treasures stored in eternity. Otherwise, man will one day live in eternal torment with those who choose not to "abide in Him." **"Let the wicked forsake his way, and the unrighteous man his thoughts: and let him return unto the Lord, and he will have mercy upon him; and to our God, for he will abundantly pardon."** (Isa. 55:7) **"And I gave her space to repent of her fornication; and she repented not. Behold, I will cast her into a bed, and them that commit adultery with her into great tribulation, except they repent of their deeds."** (Rev. 2:21,22)

Man can completely change the true meaning of Scripture by misapplication of Biblical principles. An absurd example would be for someone to quote the following verses as

Biblical truth. They are all in the Bible, but the context will tell you that to apply them in the manner presented is very wrong. **"And Judas went out and hung himself."** (Matt. 27:5) **"Go therefore and do likewise."** (Luke 10:37) **"And do so quickly."** (John 13:37) Again, as God commands in second Timothy 2:15 every person must **"Study to show thyself approved unto God . . . rightly dividing the word of truth."** God expects everyone to study the Word and not to just listen to what others may tell us the Word says.

What if a mate leaves or "puts away" a spouse?

The Bible is consistent. If an interpretation of Scripture makes a particular verse out of context with what is known Truth, it should be disregarded. Portions of I Corinthians Seven have also been used to placate those wishing to nullify God's institution of marriage. Never once in this entire chapter does the word "remarriage" appear, yet portions of it are misinterpreted by some, saying that it means that the "innocent" party in a divorce may remarry even though Paul very clearly says: **"Art thou bound unto a wife? seek not to be loosed. Art thou loosed from a wife? seek not a wife."** (I Cor. 7:27,28) He also says: **"I command, yet not I, but the Lord, Let not the wife depart from her husband: But, and if she depart, let her remain unmarried, or be reconciled to her husband: and let not the husband put away his wife."** (I Cor. 7:10,11) Those separated are nowhere told to seek another mate. Only are they told to seek reconciliation: **"be reconciled to her husband."**

Again, one-flesh mates are bound to each other for life. Those who "depart" one from the other are still husband/wife - not ex-spouses. The Divine law allows no second marriage as long as both spouses are still alive: **"The wife is bound by the law as long as her husband liveth; but if her husband be dead, she is at liberty to be married to whom she will; only in the Lord."** (I Cor. 7:39)

Another portion of this chapter deals with an "unsaved" husband or wife. This may have been put in place because of a command of the Lord that when we select a mate we are to choose a Christian: **"Be ye not unequally yoked together with unbelievers."** (II Cor. 6:14) The problem that arose was that people who called themselves Christians were trying to use this Scripture as an escape clause when they became saved saying that God would not want them to be married to a non-Christian. They would use this as an <u>unscriptural</u> reason to divorce. Again, this is Biblical heresy. Just as sex does not marry or "unmarry" two people, neither does their state of salvation. If it were so, imagine the confusion as you project the dissolutions that would take place as people fall from following the Lord and others come into a saving relationship with the Lord! The Christian calling in Paul's day didn't dissolve the marriage-covenant any more than it does today. The believer, by faith in Christ, is not loosed from an unbelieving spouse. The marriage-covenant is "for better <u>or</u> for worse."

What Paul specifically addresses is when an unbeliever leaves the believer, the believer is not under <u>bondage</u> to the deserting spouse. It is assumed that it will not be the believer who separates because of the commands from God forbidding this (unless, as previously discussed, a believer leaves for perhaps personal safety). Does this mean that those who call themselves Christians* do not divorce? With an over 50 percent divorce rate, we know that to be untrue. When an unbelieving wife or husband deserts the believer, the "innocent" party cannot physically force that person to stay. S/he must let him/her "depart." Paul adds an important fact here; that is, the person left is not under

---

*A student of the Word must be aware of the difference between a believer and an unbeliever, a "saved" Christian and an "unsaved" Christian. Many people call themselves Christians because they believe "in God," attend church, and live "good" lives (according to their standards). But a study of Scriptures tells us that if our lives do not line up with the Scriptures, we are not saved: **"He that saith I know him, <u>and</u> keepeth not his commandments, <u>is a liar</u>, and the truth is not in him."** (I John 2:4)

bondage to the person leaving.

Bondage and a marriage-covenant relationship are two entirely different things. Husbands are to **"love their wives even as Christ also loved the church and gave himself for it."** (Eph. 5:25) The husband's relationship to his wife is to be patterned after Christ's relationship to His church. This is the love to which wives are to submit: **"Wives, submit yourselves unto your own husbands, as unto the Lord."** (Eph. 5:22) If a mate chooses to leave, the other partner is not commanded to be used as a doormat by that deserting mate. Let's look at the Scriptures.

Paul takes time to address both the unbelieving wife and the unbelieving husband: **"If any brother hath a wife that believeth not, and she be pleased to dwell with him, let him not put her away. And the woman which hath a husband that believeth not, and if he be pleased to dwell with her, let her not leave him."** (I Cor. 7:12, 13) Paul continues by giving three reasons for living together. **"For the unbelieving husband is sanctified by the wife, and the unbelieving wife is sanctified by the husband: else were your children unclean; but now are they holy."** The third reason Paul gives for not physically separating is **"For what knowest thou, O wife, whether thou shalt save thy husband? or how knowest thou, O man, whether thou shalt save thy wife?"**

The Old Testament concludes with a chapter which discusses this permanence of marriage even when spouses divorce. As the Old Testament states, people were dealing "treacherously" with one another. Men had adopted corrupt principles which produced corrupt fruit. They were violating the sacred covenant of marriage by divorcing their wives and marrying others. Because of this, the Lord cut them off from his blessings. He turned from them and refused all of their offerings and false worship. He told them that they would be destroyed if they did not repent. Upset by the Lord's rejection, they came pleading for Him to find favor with them again, but they refused to repent of their sin of divorcing their wives. **"And this have ye done again, covering the altar of the Lord with tears, with weeping, and with crying out, insomuch that he regardeth not the offering** any more, or receiveth it with good will at your hand. Yet ye say, Wherefore? **Because the Lord hath been witness between thee and the wife of thy youth, against whom thou hast dealt treacherously.**" Note that the Lord recognizes the fact that they had divorced their wives, but an important principle is preserved: "**yet is she thy companion, and the wife of thy covenant.**" (Mal. 2:24)

In Chapter Two, two little words, "do" and "will" were discussed regarding the free-will decision to commit to vows and a covenant. Here again, we have a simple little word equally power-packed with meaning, "**yet.**" Study carefully its dictionary definition:

> Yet: at the present time;
> in the time still remaining;
> from the preceding time,
> as previously
> **still**

Even though they had divorced their wives, God reminded the people that His Word changes not . . . because of man's behavior . . . because of man's efforts to cover sin with worship and gifts to the church . . . with weeping or crying. His Word is "**the same yesterday, and today, and for ever.**" Divorce does not change the one-flesh covenant. In Malachi 2:14, God clearly spells this out for a permanent record for all to study:

1. She "**is thy wife**," . . . your own, bone of your bone and flesh of your flesh.
2. She "**is the wife of thy youth**," the one you chose when your affections were the strongest; your first choice.
3. She "**is thy companion**," the equal sharer in your cares, griefs, joys.
4. She "**is the wife of thy covenant**" from whom you cannot be loosed as there is an oath between you and God "so long as ye **both** shall live."

In not one of the above phrases does God use the past tense to imply that because man has "departed" or "put away" a mate that the deserted spouse is a "past-tense" mate. All verbs are present tense. Because the Lord has been the witness, regardless of what man does, s/he "**yet is.**"

The Lord continues with warnings: "**Therefore take heed to your spirit, and <u>let none deal treacherously</u> against <u>thy wife of his youth</u>**. For the Lord, The God of Israel, saith that he hateth putting away: for one covereth violence with his garment, saith the Lord of hosts: therefore take heed to your spirit, that <u>ye deal not treacherously</u> . . . Ye have wearied the Lord with your words. Yet ye say, Wherein have we wearied him? When ye say, Every one that doeth evil is good in the sight of the Lord, and he delighteth in them; or Where is the God of judgment?" God continues in Malachi Three with even stronger warnings. "<u>I will</u> come near to you to judgment; and <u>I will</u> be a swift witness against the sorcerers and against the adulterers, and against false swearers . . . For I am the Lord, <u>I change not</u>."

Man continues today saying that second, third, fourth marriages are good in the sight of the Lord, and that He delights in those who live in such a state. Some take this proof from the prosperity of such participants, but God's approval is not based upon success or failure in the world's eyes. It is based upon obedience to the Word: "**hereby know we that we are in him,**" - <u>if</u> we keep His commandments. Jesus, Himself, was deemed a failure by all of His followers and those onlookers when He was hanging nailed to a cross, stripped of all dignity, flogged and mocked, but . . . as prophecies foretold centuries before . . . "He arose, He arose, Christ Jesus, He arose!"

"Be not deceived, God will not be mocked." (Gal. 6:7) His Word is Truth: "**And he saith unto them, <u>Whosoever</u> shall put away his wife, and marry another, <u>committeth adultery</u> against her. And if a woman shall put away her husband, and be married to another, she <u>committeth adultery</u>.**" (Mark 10:11,12) "For I am the Lord, I change not"; "**Know ye not . . . adulterers . . . shall not inherit the kingdom of God.**" (Mal. 3:6; I Cor. 6:9,10)

The practice of misusing the Word is addressed by God throughout the Scriptures but especially in the last book of the Bible. "**For I testify unto every man that heareth the words of the prophecy of this book, If any man shall add unto these things, God shall add unto him the plagues that are written in this book: And if any man shall take away** from the words of the book of this prophecy, God shall take away his part out of the book of life, and out of the holy city, and from the things which are written in this book." (Rev. 22:18-19)

May God help us not to twist or add to Bible stories such as those of the woman at the well and she who was caught in the very act of adultery, to say something contrary to other clear portions or teachings of Jesus and His disciples.

"Yet ye say, Wherefore? Because the LORD hath been witness between thee and the wife of thy youth, against whom thou hast dealt treacherously: yet is she thy companion, and the wife of thy covenant. And did not he make one? Yet had he the residue of the spirit. And wherefore one? That he might seek a godly seed. Therefore take heed to your spirit, and let none deal treacherously against the wife of his youth. <u>For the LORD, the God of Israel, saith that he *hateth* putting away</u>: for one covereth violence with his garment, saith the LORD of hosts: therefore <u>take heed</u> to your spirit, that ye <u>deal not treacherously</u>."
       Malachi 2:14-16

Since the publication of this book, the Spirit of the Lord has illuminated the importance of using only the King James Bible.

CHAPTER 5
WHY WAS JOHN THE BAPTIST'S HEAD CUT OFF?

When Jesus was born in Bethlehem, King Herod ruled over the land of Israel. It was he who sent his servants to kill all the infants in Bethlehem because he hoped that among them Jesus would be killed. Several years later, King Herod died and his son succeeded him to the throne. He, like his father, was called King Herod and was likewise a wicked ruler.

The new King Herod had a brother named Philip who was married to Herodias. Herodias was a beautiful young woman and was attracted to King Herod perhaps because of his riches and power. He was likewise lured by Herodias and decided to take her from his brother Philip. Because Herod was ruler over all the land, the people approved of his actions. There followed a great celebration, a wedding feast attended by all of royalty.

There was, however, one man who did not go along with these actions, John the Baptist. John knew that in God's eyes this "marriage" was a sin that could lead to eternal death. Even though Herod was a heathen king, God's universal law concerning the institution of marriage and the rights attending it applied to him. John, a truly called prophet of God and a student of the Word, knew in his heart that he had to take upon himself the task of confronting the king as the actions represented by the highest official in the land would surely be giving a "stamp of approval" for anyone else wishing to "change partners."

For a subject of the kingdom to consider such an act of reproof was foolish in most men's eyes. After all, what right did this man have to tell the king that his marriage was illegal in God's eyes! The law of the land approved as did the royal priests who officiated at the ceremony. Even though John was fully aware of these factors, and that such action by him could cost him his freedom or even his life, he, being faithful to his calling, made the decision to speak Truth to Herod.

John the Baptist went to Herod and told him that it was a great sin to be married to someone else's wife; that God considered this relationship not a marriage but adultery. John was ridiculed and mocked. His friends turned from him for being such a fanatic. People avoided him and would no longer socialize with him. But even more alarming was the fact that Herodias, when told what John had proclaimed, was enraged. She said, "I'm so angry I could kill him," but she knew that she could not do that. Even though King Herod was not a Christian, he had heard of the fine reputation of John because of his many well-known teachings throughout the land. It was no secret to even this wicked king that John was a just and holy man. He, himself, had personally heard John teach on many occasions.

Herodias went to Herod and asked him to have John put to death. This the king refused to do, but to please his "wife" he ordered John to be bound and to be put into prison. While John was in prison, Herod's birthday came. A great feast was planned with the captains in his army and other dignitaries to be invited. Of course, there was entertainment planned with music and dancing. Now it just so happened that Herodias had a beautiful daughter named Salome who was a professional dancer. She was employed to dance before Herod and all the great men during the feast. Salome's performance so pleased the king and his guests that he wanted to reward her with something very special. Herod, being somewhat overpowered by the effects of her dancing and the fermented wine, promised to give Salome anything that she asked for. He said that even if she asked for half of his kingdom, he would give it to her. In other words, he would give her whatever she wanted.

Imagine the excitement created for this young girl regarding such an extraordinary reward! Salome went to her mother to confer about the king's generosity. Instead of suggesting that her daughter ask for precious jewels or some other material reward, Herodias immediately saw the answer to her desire for revenge toward John the Baptist. "Salome, instruct the king to send to the prison and have John the Baptist's head cut off." Salome hastened back to the king and asked as Herodias had instructed. Herod indicated that he was very sorry that he had made such a foolish promise. Even though such an oath would not be acknowledged by God, King Herod seemingly would not embarrass himself in front of his guests to save this innocent man from such a heinous, revengeful desire.

Herod sent one of his soldiers to carry out the order. The executioner beheaded John and brought his head to Salome on a large dish. She took it to her mother. Herodias was elated. Now there would be no one in all the land who would dare to speak against her "marriage" to King Herod! But . . . King Herod was reminded of John the Baptist's fate at his hands for his remaining days: " . . . **But when Herod heard thereof,** (concerning Jesus' miracles and ministry) **he said, It is John, whom I beheaded.**" (Mark 6:16)

The Story of John the Baptist from the Bible (Mark 6:17-29)

For <u>Herod</u> himself had sent forth and laid hold upon John, and bound him in prison for <u>Herodias</u>' sake, <u>his brother Philip's wife</u>: for <u>he had married her</u>. For John had said unto Herod, <u>It is not lawful</u> for thee <u>to have thy brother's wife</u>. Therefore Herodias had a quarrel against him, and would have killed him; but she could not; For Herod feared John, knowing that he was a just man and a holy, and observed him; and when he heard him, he did many things, and heard him gladly. And when a convenient day was come, that Herod on his birthday made a supper to his lords, high captains, and chief estates of Galilee; And when the daughter of the said Herodias came in, and danced, and pleased Herod and them that sat with him, the king said unto the damsel, Ask of me whatsoever thou wilt, and I will give it thee. And he sware unto her, Whatsoever thou shalt ask of me, I will give it thee, unto the half of my kingdom.

And she went forth, and said unto her mother, What shall I ask? And she said, The head of John the Baptist. And she came in straightway with haste unto the king, and asked, saying, I will that thou give me by and by in a charger the head of John the Baptist. And the <u>king was exceeding sorry; yet</u> for his oath's sake, and for their sakes which sat with him, <u>he would not reject her</u>. And immediately the king sent an executioner, and commanded his head to be brought: and he went and beheaded him in the prison, And brought his head in a charger, and gave it to the damsel: and the damsel gave it to her mother. And when his disciples heard of it, they came and took up his corpse, and laid it in a tomb."

What type of ministry did John the Baptist have?

Here was a preacher not ashamed of the gospel. John the Baptist certainly was not naive enough to not know that there would be great danger for publicly rebuking a wicked King for taking his brother's wife. Herodias was not a widow. Her husband was still living and had borne a child by Herodias. John's rebuke was not a passive suggestion but a specific charge. Royalty has no special exemptions from God's laws and John made that very clear: **"It is not lawful for thee to have her."** John was faithful but the "light" (the Word) was not welcomed in the darkness (sin) surrounding King Herod's lifestyle. Truth produced hatred. Even Herod wanted to put John to death, but he had heard many of this disciple's teachings and respected him for the word that he taught. He also feared that the people would rebel as "multitudes" had likewise heard this man's teachings and considered him a prophet of God: **"For Herod feared John, knowing that he was a just man and a holy, and observed him; and when he heard him, he did many things, and heard him gladly."** (Mark 6:20) In the book of Matthew, it is recorded that Herod would have put John to death but didn't because he feared the reaction of the people. **"For John said unto him, It is not lawful for thee to have her. And when he would have put him to death, he feared the multitude, because they counted him as a prophet."** (Matt. 14:4,5) Herod and Herodias were certainly "hearers" of the word but not "doers." Their hearts were hardened. Instead of being convicted by Truth they became embittered and compounded their sin by murder. We do not know how many people were made a part of this evildoing, but it is certain that Herodias' daughter certainly was. Here was a child who obeyed the wishes of her mother against the law of the Lord. She was entangled in the web of ungodliness and appeared to pattern her life after the lifestyle of her mother.

Historians record that John the Baptist had been in jail for about a year and a half before this insidious plan to kill him was executed. The Word will either drive people to their knees in repentance or to further rebellion. The latter happened with this royal couple. Herod with his consent to John's execution became not only an accessory, but a principal murderer. Additionally, here was a mother who instructed her own child to partake in this wicked sin - a striking out at the commandments of the Lord - **"Thou shalt not commit adultery; Thou shalt not kill."** Salome, like Eve with the serpent, could have refused to become a part of this plot to murder John; but she, too, chose the path of darkness.

King Herod pretended to be sorry that he had made the oath to give Salome her wish. He, too, could have put an end to this evil plot. A wicked oath will never justify a wicked act, but Herod tried to justify his actions because he had made an oath. One might also wonder why the many people who knew of John's reputation for being a "holy and just man" did not now come forward in his defense.

How does man react today to this same message? Does his momentary "conviction" turn to anger and to a hardened heart, or does it turn to godly sorrow which leads to true repentance with God's grace to forgive? Because man's convictions often turn to anger, most people are very careful in approaching others about sin and especially that of adultery. One would think that John the Baptist surely had to carefully search the Truth of this message before taking such a bold stand in public against the highest official in the land. Perhaps he could have saved his life if he would have said to Herod and Herodias the following:

Listen now, Herod, I'm not going to be too hard on you because after all you are not Christians. If you will just wait a few years until after Christ dies on the cross then you and your brother's wife can give your life to the Lord and 'be saved' and then can continue living in this immoral relationship the rest of your life. You will be 'new creatures in Christ.' You won't be living in sin any more. You just have to get saved, profess that you are sorry, and God will change this sin into righteousness!

John the Baptist didn't do this. He knew that God's law of marriage applies equally to everyone - Christians and non-Christians. Many like to think that if they were married and divorced before they made a commitment to the Lord that a first marriage is nullified. This irrational reasoning would mean that all unsaved people who have taken vows to a marriage-covenant are not married in God's eyes. We know that is false. John the Baptist knew this. He didn't tell these leaders to go to the church and have the previous marriage annulled or to go to the court and be awarded a divorce decree. He went to them with Truth. This marriage **"is not lawful for thee,"** because Herodias had a living spouse from a previous one-flesh covenant.

What are some Scriptures by which we can evaluate our salvation?

Many people go to church leaders and talk with them before marrying a second spouse when they have a living one-flesh mate. Those who perform ceremonies for these people often misuse Scriptures by adding what we talked about in the last chapter, "postscript rationale." Let's look at a few Scriptures which may be misinterpreted when they are taken out of context and applied to give "grace" to those whom the Scriptures say will not inherit the kingdom of God: **"Know ye not that the <u>unrighteous</u> shall not inherit the kingdom of God? Be not deceived: neither fornicators, nor idolaters, nor adulterers, nor effeminate, nor abusers of themselves with mankind, nor thieves, nor covetous nor** drunkards, nor revilers, nor extortioners, shall inherit the kingdom of God." (I Cor. 6:9,10)

"If we confess our sins, he is faithful and just to forgive us our sins, and to cleanse us from all unrighteousness." (I John 1:9) The misconception with this Scripture is that those involved in sin do not understand what "confessing" denotes. It is not an awareness of sin or being sorry for sin although these are a part of it. Note on page 69 that Herod was very much **aware** of wrong-doing. **"And the king was exceeding sorry."** But, he did not repent - turn from doing what he knew was wrong. **"Yet for his oath's sake, and for their sakes which sat with him, he would not reject her. And immediately the king sent an executioner, and commanded his head to be brought."** Confession involves turning from sin. If we acknowledge that an act is sin then we must realize that God hates sin and that we must not love what He hates else we are not in fellowship with Him. Read further in I John. **"And hereby we do know that we know him, if we keep his commandments. He that saith, I know him, and keepeth not his commandments, is a liar and the truth is not in him."** (I John 2:3,4) **"Thou shalt not commit adultery, Thou shalt not kill, Thou shalt not steal, Thou shalt not bear false witness, Thou shalt not covet . . ."** (Rom. 13:9)

Another Scripture falsely applied is I John 2:25: **"And this is the promise that he hath promised us, even eternal life."** Again refer to the Scriptures above. The Lord's will is that none shall perish, but many do. Those who perish do so because they choose to follow false teachings or rebel against what they know the Word says. **"Whosoever transgresseth,** (violates, breaks) **and abideth not in the doctrine** (that which is taught) **of Christ, hath not God."** Second Peter, Chapter Two, gives strong warnings regarding the doctrines of false prophets, teachers, and to those who have fallen and who will fall prey to such abominations to the Lord: **"But there were false prophets also among the people, even as there shall be false teachers among you, who privily shall bring in damnable heresies, even denying the Lord that bought them, and bring upon themselves swift destruction."** (2 Pet. 2:1,2) Study carefully this entire chapter of II Peter. It continues to describe many of those who do not teach what the Bible says. They sometimes are involved in the very sins that, in their blasphemy, they say are honored by God: **"having eyes full of adultery, and that cannot cease from sin; beguiling unstable souls . . . which have forsaken the right way, and are gone astray . . . they allure through the lusts of the flesh . . . while they promise them liberty, they themselves are the servants of corruption: for of whom a man is overcome, of the same is he brought in bondage."** (2 Pet. 2:14-19) This message in the New Testament regarding false teaching is the same as that in the Old. **"Woe be unto the pastors that destroy and scatter the sheep of my pasture! saith the Lord . . . Mine heart within me is broken, because of the prophets . . . I have seen also in the prophets of Jerusalem a horrible thing: they commit adultery, and walk in lies: they strengthen also the hands of evil doers, that none doth return from his wickedness: they are all of them unto me as Sodom, and the inhabitants thereof as Gomorrah."** (Jer. 23:1, 9, 14,15)

Another promise from the Lord which is at times misapplied is from Colossians: " **. . . having forgiven you all trespasses . . ." (Col. 2:13)** God does cancel trespasses for all who repent and believe - that the Word is true. We have two free-will choices with sin: to part from it - stop it, or to perish in it. The Old Testament books of Hosea and Jeremiah tell us of God's will and his actions of agape love as he waits not to bring into the kingdom those who persist in murdering, stealing, swearing, and committing adultery but to receive those who hate sin and are willing to turn from it and thus receive His forgiveness - blotting out our transgressions. (Hosea 4:2)

We are not condemned by the Word if we follow the Word. That promise is given in Romans the eighth chapter. **"There is therefore now no condemnation to them which are in Christ Jesus, who walk not after the flesh, but after the Spirit."** To be "in Christ," you cannot walk after the flesh. The works of the flesh are clearly defined in Galatians 5:10-21. **"Now the works of the flesh are manifest, which are these: adultery, fornication . . . idolatry, witchcraft**

. . . **murders, drunkenness** . . . **they which do such things shall not inherit the kingdom of God.**" Man erroneously only quotes the first clause of Romans 8:1, "**There is therefore now no condemnation to them which are in Christ Jesus,**" implying that the Lord does not condemn anyone who confesses to be a "saved" Christian regardless of their immoral behavior. They completely ignore the included condition - **if** you "**walk not after the flesh.**" This Scripture is often tied to II Corinthians 5:17: "**Therefore if any man be in Christ, he is a new creature: old things are passed away; behold, all things are become new.**" Man infers that when he becomes a Christian, God forgives him of all past sin and the slate is wiped clean. This is true . . . in part; God does forgive us of any past sin . . . **but only** if we repent - turn from that sin. Note the "condition" **if** we are "new creatures," we stop doing those "old" things which are considered sin in God's eyes. The test is whether or not we have turned from these old habits. For example, if before I became a Christian, my profession was prostitution or drugs, I cannot continue in those lifestyles and be considered saved - according to the Scriptures. Even though a person may say that he didn't understand that prostitution was wrong before, he cannot continue committing those acts that make a person a prostitute or drug addict.

People try to use this "scapegoat" to excuse them in an adulterous marriage saying that <u>before</u> they were saved they divorced and married a second spouse, but now they are new creatures in Christ, and all things are passed away. They imply that God doesn't "count" the first marriage as valid because they didn't know God's law. Surely God will extend a "second chance." No, God didn't modify sin for Herod, and He doesn't for man today. "**He is no respector of persons.**" God's second, third, or fourth chance is His grace to bring the Truth - the Word - to the entire world and to give man the free-will choice to receive it in obedience or to reject it in rebellion.

How are repentance and baptism related?

Repent and be baptized - this was John the Baptist's

message; it was the message of the disciples; it was the message and is the message of Jesus Christ. Baptism, like grace, does not change sin into righteousness. Those who obey the command **"repent and be baptized"** should <u>first</u> turn from sin - outwardly and inwardly. The acknowledgment of knowing Him is that we keep His commandments. This public affirmation declares to all that the participant has made a decision to walk according to the Word.

Some who are baptized do so knowing they are living in sin; others repent of known sin but later apostatize. Simon Magnus was such an example. We are told of him in the eighth chapter of Acts. He made a solemn profession of repentance for his sin, turned from it, was baptized, and appeared to faithfully follow Biblical teachings; however, his heart had not been circumcised. Peter some time later declared to him: **"Thy money <u>perish with thee</u>, because thou hast thought that the gift of God may be purchased with money. Thou hast neither part nor lot in this matter: for thy <u>heart is not right</u> in the sight of God. Repent therefore of this thy wickedness, and pray God, if perhaps the <u>thought</u> of thine heart may be forgiven thee. For I perceive that <u>thou art</u> in the <u>gall</u> of bitterness, and in the <u>bond</u> of iniquity."** (Acts 8:20-23) (Indwelling sin is a root of bitterness **"that beareth gall and wormwood."**) (Deu. 29:18)

Simon had obtained a good name among God's people; he put on a form of godliness among them, but Peter exposed his wickedness. This disciple told Simon, **"Thou hast neither part nor lot in this matter."** The apostate did not have Truth. His <u>heart</u> was not right in the sight of God and he would not receive the eternal benefits of God's grace . . . unless he truly repented. He could not make excuses for his sin implying that it was done in innocence. To continue manifesting a sin by making excuses for it once it has been exposed is even more evidence of the signs of a hardened heart and a reprobate mind. **"Let no man say when he is tempted, I am tempted of God: for God cannot be tempted with evil, neither tempteth he any man: But every man is tempted, when he is drawn away of his own lust, and enticed. Then when lust hath conceived, it bringeth forth sin: and**

sin, when it is finished, bringeth forth death. Do not err, my beloved brethren."* (Jas. 1:13-16) Simon was told three things:
1. to repent
2. to be baptized
3. to pray

We should all pray fervently before the Lord that His grace will be extended in all of our transgressions and that we will not harden our hearts against true repentance and be turned over to a reprobate mind to continue in sin with a seared conscience. **"For godly sorrow worketh repentance to**

---

*Transgressors become in **bondage** to sin (**"in the bond of iniquity"**) by repetition of sin. Perhaps an analogy to the production of silk may help the reader to visualize the danger of telling a **little** white lie, of **just** looking at another person with lust, of planning **one day** to get right with the Lord. Natural silk is produced by a caterpillar. It creates this most beautiful fiber within its own body. The silk filament is extruded through a tube in its head called a spinneret. The caterpillar spins a cocoon by throwing this self-made filament around its body in a figure-eight motion with its head. The spinning continues until the animal, now a moth, has completely encased itself with this beautiful fiber. It then produces another secretion which enables it to cut through the cocoon to fly away to "freedom." However, if permitted to emerge from the chrysalis, the moth by cutting through the end of the cocoon would damage the continuous filament. To prevent this, the moth with its cocoon, is killed by placing it in boiling water or by freezing. Man then unwinds the silk filament and discards the "creator." Humans, too, **wrap** themselves - with sin - "thread by thread" with seemingly insignificant trespasses, until they are "encased" by a rope (in the bond of iniquity) from which there is very little probability of escape. We become in bondage to not only the original sin but many other accompanying ones . . . **"and shall utterly perish in their** (our) **own corruption."** (II Pet. 2:12)

salvation not to be repented of: but the sorrow of the world worketh death." (II Cor. 7:10)

Many have preached: **"Repent, and be baptized every one of you in the name of Jesus Christ for the remission of sins."** (Acts 2:38) The disciples preached this message and were persecuted for it. John the Baptist preached repentance and was beheaded. Jesus Christ preached repentance and was hung on a cross. Man, however, cannot "kill" the Word. It lives on forever. Man can only rebel against It. That is the love of God in giving every person a free-will choice; and a second, third, fourth chance – to repent. He is waiting to forgive, to receive anyone who will turn from sin and to Him no matter how perverted a lifestyle has become. **"Even so it is not the will of your Father which is in heaven, that one of these little ones should perish."** But we do know that many have, do, and will perish as they **"depart from the faith, giving heed to seducing spirits, and doctrines of devils. Speaking lies in hypocrisy; having their conscience seared with a hot iron."** (I Tim. 4:1,2)

Every person is responsible not only for obeying the Word but to take it in truth to others. Each person is a watchman to **"rightly divide the word of truth"** for himself and to "blow the trumpet" (tell others) so that when the "sword" (death) does come s/he will not have others' "blood" on his/her hands: **"Then whosoever heareth the sound of the trumpet, and taketh not warning; if the sword come, and take him away, his blood shall be upon his own head. He heard the sound of the trumpet, and took not warning; his blood shall be upon him. But he that taketh warning shall deliver his soul. But if the watchman see the sword come, and blow not the trumpet, and the people be not warned; if the sword come, and take any person from among them, he is taken away in his iniquity; but his blood will I require at the watchman's hand . . . When I say unto the wicked, O wicked man, thou shalt surely die; if thou dost not speak to warn the wicked from his way, that wicked man shall die in his iniquity; but his blood will I require at thine hand. Nevertheless, if thou warn the wicked of his way to turn from it; if he do not turn from his way, he shall die in his** __iniquity;__ but thou hast delivered thy soul." (Ezel. 33:4-9)

EPILOGUE

The illustration of John the Baptist in this chapter may be more graphic than most would want to accept, but it is based upon a true story depicting the horrible results of lust, sin, hardened hearts, and seared consciences. Herodias became so corrupt with self-desires that she had no qualms about making even her own daughter a part of her horrible revenge. We must not become so "separated" by time with Biblical accounts that we forget that real people with feelings and hardships have gone before us. Their lives are examples for us to study so that we will not make the same mistakes.

John the Baptist paid a big price to say to his contemporaries and to his ruling non-Christian King: **"It is not lawful for thee to have thy brother's wife"**! This was the Lord's beloved disciple who was sent with a message that was not heeded in that day. Because the people who heard the Word, did not submit to It, did not make the Word any less true. Those who know the reason for John the Baptist's death should, if nothing else, look very carefully at the message that he carried to his grave.

When we hear this message of repentance, does it cause our hearts to respond gladly and freely, or like Herod and Herodias, do we react with resentment?

"Have mercy upon me, O God, according to thy loving-kindness: according unto the multitude of thy tender mercies blot out my transgressions. Wash me thoroughly from mine iniquity, and cleanse me from my sin. For __I acknowledge my transgressions__ . . . against thee, and thee only, have I sinned, and done this evil in thy sight . . . Behold, thou desirest truth __in the inward parts__ . . . Restore unto me the joy of thy salvation; and uphold me with thy free spirit . . . __Then__ will I teach transgressors thy ways; and sinners shall be converted unto thee." (Psa. 51)

CHAPTER 6
DID DAVID AND BATHSHEBA GET AWAY WITH ADULTERY?

The story of David and Bathsheba has been misinterpreted by many to defend the sin of adultery. It has not, however, been inappropriately used to justify the sin of murder - a transgression also committed by David to cover up his sin of adultery. On the other side of this paradoxical situation is that both of these trespasses were not uncommon for men in leadership.

What was the purpose for which the Lord chose to record this incident out of the millions of stories which could have been recorded in the Old Testament? Would the Lord's purpose have been that man might use this example as a pattern for lifestyles of society today? Rational thinking should certainly rule this out! First, one must look at the times. Concubines were "acceptable" in man's sight; even David had many wives and concubines. Kings routinely sent men into battle who were killed. David sent Uriah, Bathsheba's husband and a loyal soldier, into battle. Uriah was killed in combat.

What David did regarding Uriah was completely in his "right" as a king. He could send any man into the field to fight. Why, then, did God call this murder when never before was David accused of this sin for the thousands of others whom he had sent into battle and were killed in the line of duty? Why did God make an issue of David's affair with Bathsheba and Uriah's death? Could it be that God chose to permanently record this episode for people of all ages not to give his approval of adultery and murder, but for the following reasons:
   1. to show the danger of what we secretly desire inwardly (heart attitudes): **"But I say unto you,**

that whosoever <u>looketh</u> on a woman <u>to lust</u> after her hath <u>committed adultery</u> with her already <u>in his heart</u>." (Matt. 5:28) "And an evil man out of the <u>evil treasure of his heart</u> bringeth forth that which is evil." (Luke 6:45) "Do not ye yet understand . . . those things which proceed out of the mouth <u>come forth</u> <u>from the heart;</u> and they defile the man. For <u>out of the heart</u> proceed evil thoughts, murders, adulteries, fornications, thefts, false witness, blasphemies: These are the things which defile a man." (Matt. 15:17-20)

2. to show the horrible effects of adultery on families;
3. that even people called by God to serve and be used mightily will fall prey to the **wages** of sin if they do not daily confess and repent (abhor and turn from what God calls sin);
4. that when man doesn't repent by turning from sin, his conscience becomes so seared that he no longer has a sense of right or wrong: **"Speaking lies in hypocrisy; having their <u>conscience seared</u> with a hot iron."** (I Tim. 4:2);
5. that when man refuses to obey the Word, God, <u>as part of His judgment</u>, permits him to live in his sin: **"God gave them over to a <u>reprobate mind</u> . . . being filled with all unrighteousness, fornication, wickedness, maliciousness; full of envy, murder, debate, malignity, whisperers, backbiters, haters of God, despiteful, proud, boasters, inventors of evil things, disobedient to parents, <u>covenant-breakers</u>, without natural affection."** God continues by stating that these people once knew better but persisted in rebellion (sin) and now **"have pleasure"** in **encouraging** others to join them. (Rom. 1:24-32)

The Old Testament was written <u>for us</u> that we would study <u>and</u> avoid the error of man in the past; the New Testament was written <u>to us</u>, that each of us would have a concise record of how we are to conduct our lives today. Many of the customs, rituals, and ceremonies of the peoples represented in the Old Testament do not apply to us today, but the principles of obedience and trust in the Lord are the same throughout history. For example, under the Old Testament law, polygamy was permitted by man: Solomon had 300 wives and 700 concubines. Shall we say that under "grace" today, that we are to encourage this type of living because man allowed it in the past? We know this to be wrong. "Grace" is God's provision of mercy for repentant sinners. It is not a "license" to live in sin. Laws were given to regulate sin; but in giving of these ordinances, the accompanying sins were not sanctioned by the Lord. God did not approve of slavery, but laws were adopted which regulated it. He did not approve of man's disputes, but regulations were sanctioned to settle them.

Likewise, God has never approved of murder, sodomy, drunkenness, or adultery. Because man sins and even perhaps appears to "get away" with it, does not change God's standards. As Jesus told the Pharisees who came to Him with the sole purpose of trapping Him into agreeing with the sin of adultery: **"What did Moses command you? And they said, Moses suffered to write a bill of divorcement, and to put her away. And Jesus answered and said unto them, For the hardness of your heart he wrote you this precept.**" The Lord told them that Moses wrote this because man refused to repent from the sins giving rise to divorce. (We also saw in the third chapter of this book that the "bill of divorcement" publicly "cleared" the "put-away" spouse of sexual sin as the punishment for such was death by stoning.) Jesus continued to repeat for the Pharisees the Truth which they already knew in their heart: **"But from the beginning of the creation God made them male and female . . ."** The Lord concluded by stating how He looks at the marriage to a second mate when there is a living one-flesh spouse: **"Whosoever shall put away his wife, and marry another, committeth adultery against her. And if a woman shall put away her husband, and be married to another, she committeth adultery."** (Mark 10:3-6,11,12) God has never agreed with adultery, or murder, or sodomy, or stealing. Just because provisions are made to deal with man's hard-heartedness does not mean that God then says that the accompanying sinful behavior is excused in His eyes.

In our own country today, there are over one million divorces every year; over 20,000 <u>reported</u> murderers, and over three million <u>reported</u> robberies. During the Holocaust under Hitler, over eleven million Jews and non-Jews were murdered. Because these things have been "allowed" by God, are we to interpolate by saying that "under grace" today, we are to encourage and accept this type of living and that God approves? A seemingly absurd statement, but man daily twists God's word to excuse sinful behavior relating to the institution of marriage saying that God "allows" it, or that God "allowed" it in times past.

Conversely, it appears what has happened is that we as a nation are reaping the seeds of destruction which have been sown little by little throughout our country. There are natural laws and Divine laws. We are familiar, for example, of the law of gravity. If we jump off a building, we will fall to the ground. Our free-will act to leap from such a height is our decision. We have been taught from childhood that if we do certain things, we will be hurt. Hopefully, lessons taught by parents regarding such warnings will be heeded. Likewise, do we have Divine laws. If we transgress these, we are told by God what will happen. One of these given throughout Scriptures is that if we continue to sin we will:

    1. become in bondage to that sin
    2. be turned over to a reprobate mind

The second of the above repercussions of rebellion, some may say is "unfair." But like the law of gravity, God, our Father, warns us. He tells us that repetition of a sin results in our mind being controlled by that sin to a point where we can no longer distinguish right from wrong. We then see wrong as right and right as wrong. When this happens God's judgment is at hand. Review point five on page 81 for identifiable characteristics of people living in the "harvest" of reprobate minds: **"being filled with all unrighteousness, fornication, wickedness, maliciousness; full of envy, murder, debate, malignity, whisperers, backbiters, haters of God, dispiteful, proud, boasters, inventors of evil things, disobedient to parents,** covenant-breakers, without natural affection." (Rom. 1:24-32) We have become a people **speaking lies in hypocrisy; having** (our) **their conscience seared with a hot iron."** (I Tim. 4:2)

Why should we study the Old Testament?

By studying the lives of the prophets, leaders, and families of the Bible, we can learn to avoid the same mistakes others have made, <u>or</u> we can perhaps project the potential "reaping" from historical examples if we choose to rebel against God's principles - just as man did in past years. Here was a man, David, an honored king through whose line the promised Messiah would come. The Lord at one time called David "a man after his own heart," yet he was a person who lied, who committed adultery, who murdered. Does this seem possible?

God does not conceal sin. He does not record it for our imitation, but for our admonition. He shows that the greatest of man can fall folly to temptation and thus warns us **"Let him that thinks he stands take heed lest he fall."** Man must make a concerted effort to remain pure before the Lord. Sin must immediately be confessed and repented of - turned from, stopped, else we be destroyed by it, as was Saul whom the Lord described as: **"a choice young man, and a goodly; and there was not among the children of Israel a goodlier person than he."** (I Sam. 9:2) Saul, however, turned his heart from obeying the commands of the Lord and had his kingdom taken from him, dying "with a tormenting spirit." Another leader, the Pharoah, ruler over Egypt, was given ten specific, recorded opportunities, to repent. The Lord "under grace" sent His foremost ranking "ambassador," Moses, repeatedly to plead with this wicked leader to turn from his maliciousness. But, the Pharoah, too, refused, each time "hardening his heart," until he and thousands of his followers were finally destroyed in the Red Sea. (Psa. 136:15) Too late, they realized, **"the wages of sin is death!"**

Like the woman at the well and the woman caught in adultery, the story of David and Bathsheba has been misapplied, sometimes out of ignorance, but more often out of a desire to justify sin. To better understand the significance behind the lifestyle of this man who transgressed God's commandments, **"thou shalt not commit adultery, Thou shalt not kill, Thou shalt not bear false witness, Thou shalt not covet . . ."** we must look not only at the events giving rise to his adultery, but to other related incidents providing the woven tapestry of David's life.

Why did God choose David to become a king?

God chose David to be king when he was a young boy, seemingly least favored among all of the sons of his father, Jesse. Samuel, God's servant, was sent to anoint David as king: **". . . fill thine horn with oil, and go, I will send thee to Jesse the Bethlehemite: for I have provided me a king among his sons."** (I Sam. 16:1) Each of Jesse's sons was presented to Samuel as one whom God might choose because of his height, stature, or appearance; but God had forewarned Samuel: **"Look not on his countenance, or on the height of his stature; because I have refused him; man looketh on the outward appearance, but the <u>Lord looketh on the heart.</u>"** (I Sam. 16,7)

Finally, after the process of elimination, whereby each of Jesse's sons was presented but rejected, David was called from the field. **"And he sent, and brought him in. Now he was ruddy and withal of a beautiful countenance, and goodly to look to. And the Lord said, Arise, anoint him: for this is he."** (I Sam. 16:12) David was anointed to become the king to replace Saul, but first he was to serve this king under most unpleasant circumstances.

The above honor was bestowed on David just after God had announced to Saul that he was sorry that He had made him king, for Saul had refused to obey God's commands. Here again this same prophet, Samuel, had been sent as God's messenger to talk with Saul about his disobedience, but he was still unrepentant. He confessed his sin and presented offerings and sacrifices, but his heart was not changed. Outwardly he appeared to have repented, but God knew his evil heart. Samuel told King Saul that the Lord's favor had been removed and of His displeasure. **"For rebellion is as the sin of witchcraft, and stubbornness is as iniquity and idolatry. Because thou hast <u>rejected the word of the Lord</u>, he hath also rejected thee from being king.** (I Sam. 15:23) Saul tried to "play" the same game that Adam and Eve had in their making excuses for their sin. He had disobeyed the Lord. Samuel told him so. Instead of repenting, Saul continued in self-deception: **"I have obeyed the voice of the Lord . . . But the people took of the spoil, sheep and oxen . . . "** (I Sam. 15:20-21) This is why another king was chosen. God said: **"It repenteth me that I have set up Saul to be king: for he is turned back from following me, and <u>hath not performed my commandments</u>."** (I Sam. 15:11) As additional punishment: **"the spirit of the Lord departed from Saul, and an evil spirit from the Lord troubled him."** (I Sam. 16:14)

Saul was so despondent that his aides suggested that they find a harpist to play for him. David was called and was so effective in "quieting" Saul's tormenting spirit that he was asked to join the king's staff. So we see the beginning of God's hand upon David, already a favored servant of the king and a gifted musician. David's talents did not end here. As he grew in stature and obedience to the Lord we also find him stepping out to conquer the great enemy of the Israelites, the Philistines.

This greatly feared foe was led by the giant Goliath. David went to Saul and told him that he would "take care of Goliath." Saul, of course, told him how foolish his offer was, but David insisted, and as the story is recorded . . . David slew Goliath with a stone hurled from his sling. This won for David an appointment as Saul's special assistant. He always carried out his assignments successfully and was promoted to commander of Saul's troops. People, however, began cheering both Saul and David: "Saul has slain his thousands, and David his ten thousands!" Saul became jealous and remarked, "next, they'll be making him their king." Saul's fits of rage increased as did his physical attacks against David. The king began throwing his spear at David when he would play the harp and finally banned him from his presence and demoted him to the rank of captain. David, however, prospered even more in the eyes of the people.

Saul began to conspire to kill David; first by sending him into battle where he was certain that David would be killed, then by personally pursuing him with his best troops. Through all of this David honored Saul and did not try to defend himself by retaliating against his king. He lived a life pleasing to the Lord, humble in his spirit, repentant in his living, and obedient to the tasks set before him. Under "Divine law," David was to be faithful unto Saul as long as this king lived. In exasperation Saul decided to offer him his daughter for his wife if he would go to battle, hoping that David's life would be taken. David agreed but was victorious on the battlefield. He expressed his humble feelings for such an honor - to be the king's son-in-law. Plans were made for the wedding. However, when the time arrived for the ceremony, Saul instead gave his daughter in marriage to another man. Again, he went to David and now offered him his youngest daughter. David was honored, but asked how a poor man like him from an unknown family could find enough dowry to marry the daughter of a king. Another opportunity for Saul to get rid of David presented itself. King Saul responded by telling this faithful servant that the only dowry he needed was 100 dead Philistines, hoping that David would be killed in the battle. Again, God was with David, and he paid his dowry with his war trophies. So Saul gave Michal to David for his wife, but this only further deepened the hatred of Saul for David.

For some five to ten years, we see David being pursued by the king and his army. Only once did David retaliate. In a cave, he slipped up behind Saul and quietly slit off the bottom of his robe, but immediately his conscience began bothering him. He repented: "It is a serious sin to attack God's chosen king in any way." He arose and went out of the cave and cried after Saul, saying **"My lord the king. And when Saul looked behind him, David stooped with his face to the earth, and bowed himself."** (I Sam. 24)

How did David bring judgment upon himself?

In I Samuel, Chapter Twenty-five, we are told that Saul forced his daughter Michal, David's wife, to marry another man. Also recorded is David's taking additional wives for himself, Abigal and Ahinoam. More wives continued to be added to the list: Maacah, Adonijah, Haggith, Shephatiah, and Ithream, to name only a few, plus now we also read about David's concubines. Somewhere, a change in "heart" took place within David. The manifestation of this we see in his outward behavior. (It is not possible for man to live in a lifestyle characterized by sin and have a pure heart toward God. One or the other will prevail. **"Be not deceived, God is not mocked."** [Gal. 6:7])

Let's look at a changed David, one who gave into temptation and did not "pluck out" his sinful eye: **"And if thy right eye offend thee, pluck it out, and cast it from thee: for it is profitable for thee that one of thy members should perish, and not that thy whole body should be cast into hell."** (Matt. 5:29) The account of this disastrous departure from keeping a pure heart before the Lord is recorded in the eleventh chapter of II Samuel.

David became a popular, wealthy king and a great warrior. This was after Saul had killed himself subsequent to being defeated in a battle with the Philistines. With Saul no longer alive, the Lord had instructed David to take his place as king. He ruled well and fought many victorious battles. However, at a particular period in David's reign, we find him digressing from his normal responsibilities: **"And it came to pass, after the year was expired, at the time when kings go forth to battle, that David sent Joab, and his servants with him, and all Israel; and they destroyed the children of Ammon, and besieged Rabbah. <u>But David tarried still at Jerusalem.</u> And it came to pass in an eveningtide, that David arose from off his bed, and walked upon the roof of the king's house: and from the roof he saw a woman washing herself; and the woman was very beautiful to look upon."** It was not uncommon to bathe on the rooftop. Only a building such as the palace would tower above the normal roof lines.

David made a great error in not rejecting the natural fleshly desire to look upon female nakedness from "another well." We are given examples of men who were also tempted, but had sexual lust under control by **actively** resisting it. Job was one who said: **"I made a covenant with mine eyes; why then should I think upon a maid?** (Job 31:1); and Joseph who was thrown into jail and stripped of his rank in the kingdom because he refused to sleep with his master's reputedly beautiful wife: **"And it came to pass after these things, that his master's wife cast her eyes upon Joseph; and she said, Lie with me. But he refused, and said unto his master's wife, Behold my master wotteth not what is with me in the house, and he hath committed all that he hath to my hand; There is none greater in this house than I; neither hath he kept back any thing from me but thee, because thou art his wife: how then can I do this great wickedness, and sin against God?** (Gen. 39:7-9) Those that love God do, for this latter reason, hate sin. The king's wife persisted; she came each day to him and offered herself, but Joseph continued to reject this temptation. His pious resolve greatly angered her, so she fabricated an affair with Joseph and called to the servants of the house to come to her rescue and have this loyal servant cast into prison. (Gen. 39)

David, however, did not have his mind set to resist sexual temptation: **"But every man is tempted, when he is drawn away of his own lust, and enticed. Then when lust hath conceived, it bringeth forth sin: and sin, when it is finished, bringeth forth death."** (Jas. 1:14,15) Instead of turning from his lust, David continued to watch and decided he would like to have this woman for himself. "Who is this woman?" inquired David. The reply was that she was Bathsheba, the wife of Uriah, one of his faithful soldiers. David, having entertained "lust" in his heart, determined to have this woman even though she was already married to Uriah. "Bring Bathsheba to me," he commanded. This was accomplished: **"And David sent messengers, and took her; and she came in unto him, and he lay with her . . . and she returned unto her house.** One thing David had not counted upon - being caught! **"And the woman conceived, and sent and** told David, and said, I am with child." (II Sam. 11:4,5)

Here again, we see David rejecting the Lord by rebellion in not confessing his sin and turning from it. He instead thought of a great cover-up: immediately bring Uriah home from battle and have him sleep with Bathsheba so that he would think the child was his: **"And David sent to Joab, saying, Send me Uriah the Hittite. And Joab sent Uriah to David. And when Uriah was come unto him, David demanded of him how Joab did, and how the people did, and how the war prospered.** David very carefully tried to entice Uriah to manifest his physical affections to his wife. **"And David said to Uriah, Go down to thy house, and wash thy feet. And Uriah departed out of the king's house, and there followed him a mess of meat from the king."**

The military custom of the times dictated that when a man was assigned to be in battle, he was not to sleep with his wife. Here, David knowing the normal sexual desire of man for his wife, and Uriah having been away from his wife for some time, was quite certain that he would sleep with Bathsheba and have sexual relations. (A modern scene would include a motel room with wine and a gourmet dinner being sent to the room!) <u>**But Uriah slept at the door of the king's house with all the servants of his lord, and went not down to his house.**</u> David had not anticipated the fact that Uriah was indeed a devoted, obedient soldier and would not subject himself to this "misconduct." David's servants reported back to him: **"Uriah went not down unto his house."** So David called Uriah before him and said: **"Camest thou not from thy journey? why then didst thou not go down unto thine house?**

And Uriah said unto David, "The ark, and Israel, and Judah, abide in tents; and my lord Joab, and the servants of my lord, are encamped in the open fields; shall I then go into mine house, to eat and to drink, and to lie with my wife? as thou livest, and as thy soul liveth, I will not do this thing." What was David to do now? What in the world was wrong with this man, anyway!

David's next plan of action was to lure Uriah into getting drunk and then perhaps under his stupor he would weaken and return to his wife: **"And David said to Uriah,**

Tarry here today also, and tomorrow, I will let thee depart. So Uriah abode in Jerusalem that day, and the morrow. And when David had called him, he did eat and drink before him; and he made him drunk: and at even he went out to lie on his bed with the servants of his lord, but went not down to his house."

Foiled again! David, having been given much opportunity to confess his sin, still refused. Instead, he put himself deeper in the mire by instructing Joab, his commander in chief, to place Uriah in a position where he would be killed. For a king to order someone into battle was a "right" and attached to it was not any misdoing. Perhaps David had learned this "trick of the trade" from Saul who had, several years earlier, sent him into battle hoping that he would be killed. **"And he wrote a letter, saying Set ye Uriah in the forefront of the hottest battle, and retire ye from him, that he may be smitten and die. And it came to pass, when Joab observed the city, that he assigned Uriah unto a place where he knew that valiant men were. And the men of the city went out, and fought with Joab: and there fell some of the people of the servants of David; and Uriah the Hittite died also."** Joab sent word to David about the battle and all of the men who were killed, including Uriah. Joab's message expressed concern about Uriah's death. David, still masking his sin replied: **"Let not this thing displease thee, for the sword devoureth one as well as another: make thy battle more strong against the city, and overthrow it,"** implying that this was a chance of war, only a common thing that happened to Uriah.

Bathsheba was notified of her husband's death and went into mourning. When that time was past, **"David sent and fetched her to his house, and she became his wife, and bare him a son."** The sin was exposed. David had pleased himself . . . but **"the thing that David had done displeased the Lord"**: the adultery, falsehood, murder, and this marriage. God sees and hates sin, especially in his own people. From this day forth until David's death, tragedy continually plagued his house and his children.

David had lived with his unrepented sin for at least nine months when God sent the prophet Nathan to relate a parable that brought David to his knees. We can estimate the approximate time as the Scriptures relate that the child conceived of this illicit relationship had been born. The parable contrasted a rich man who had many flocks and herds and a poor man who had nothing except one lamb which had grown up with him and his children and was a family pet. The rich man entertained a guest from out of town and wanted to impress him. Instead of slaughtering one of the many lambs from his personal flock, he took this nurtured lamb from the poor man and used it for a feast with his guest. David was furious about this great injustice and commanded that this man should die for such an heinous act. Nathan replied, **"Thou art the man."** David immediately knew the foolishness of his actions and heard the Lord's voice; his consciousness of sin returned. For his **taking of another's wife** and murder, death was the sentence; the transgressor knew this. What David had done, however, was camouflaged by his position as king. In man's eyes, as ruler over the land, he had not committed "capital" crimes. But God judges by the heart, and King David was guilty.

How did David's sin affect his family?

Sin goes beyond the one committing the transgression. With adultery, for example, families are destroyed and many accompanying relationships. Lifestyles set by parents are often not only frequently duplicated by children but are intensified in excesses. **"Thus saith the Lord God of Israel, I anointed thee king over Israel, and I delivered thee out of the hand of Saul; And I gave thee thy master's house, and thy master's wives into thy bosom, and gave thee the house of Israel and of Judah; and if that had been too little, I would moreover have given unto thee such and such things. Wherefore** <u>hast thou despised the commandment of the Lord</u>, **to do evil in his sight?** <u>thou hast killed Uriah</u> **the Hittite with the sword,** <u>and hast taken his wife to be thy wife</u>, **and hast slain him with the sword of the children of Ammon.** The Lord makes it very clear to this king that he knows what David has done. He then proceeds to pass sentence upon him: **"Now therefore the sword shall never** depart from thine house;" and why? "because thou hast despised me, and hast taken the wife of Uriah the Hittite to be thy wife. Thus said the Lord Behold:

> I will raise up evil against thee out of thine own house.
>
> I will take thy wives before thine eyes and give them unto thy neighbor, and he shall lie with thy wives in the sight of this sun.
>
> Thou didst it secretly: but I will do this thing before all Israel, and before the sun."

"And David said unto Nathan, I have sinned against the Lord." Nathan continued to talk with David adding that he had also "given great occasion to the enemies of the Lord to blaspheme" and because of this his child would die. David had within a few short moments laid before him his sowing and reaping. Oh, for the brief period of sexual pleasure, if only he had not determined in his heart to err! "Then when lust hath conceived, it bringeth forth sin: and sin, when it is finished, bringeth forth death. Do not err, my beloved brethren." (Jas. 1:15,16)

"And the Lord struck the child that Uriah's wife bare unto David, and it was very sick." David prayed and fasted and was deeply sorry for his transgressions. Priests and others surrounding him joined in the petitions to the Lord, but to no avail. The child died.

The Lord continued to physically protect David in battle, but family tragedy heightened and was his lot from that day forth. Amnon, one of David's sons, became attracted to his half-sister, Tamar. He verbalized this "love" for her to his friends. They, instead of admonishing him and reproving this act of lust, helped him in feigning an illness and asking that Tamar be permitted to come to cook and care for him. David, not knowing Amnon's intentions, arranged to have his daughter sent to Amnon. "So Tamar went to her brother Amnon's house; and he was laid down. And she took flour, and kneaded it, and made cakes in his sight, and did bake the cakes." Amnon dismissed the servants and called to his sister. When she answered his call, he grabbed her arm trying to force her to go to bed with him. "**Come lie with me, my sister. And she answered him, Nay, my brother, do not force me; for no such thing ought to be done in Israel: do not thou this folly.**" (II Sam. 13)

She pleaded reminding her brother what a serious crime it would be and asking him where she would go in her shame. She continued to tell Amnon that for him this "affair" would just be laughed off "with the boys" but for her, this ignominy would ever go with her: "**And I, whether shall I cause my shame to go? and as for thee, thou shalt be as one of the fools in Israel,**" but he wouldn't listen to her and "**he forced her, and lay with her.**" This innocent virgin was disgraced for her remaining days for this vile act of lust which immediately turned to hatred in many aspects. "**He would not hearken unto her voice: but, being stronger than she, forced her, and lay with her. Then Amnon said unto her, Arise, be gone. And she said unto him, There is no cause: this evil in sending me away is greater than the other that thou didst unto me. But he would not hearken unto her. Then he called his servant that ministered unto him, and said, Put now this woman out from me, and bolt the door after her.**"

Absalom, a favored brother of Tamar, took her in where she lived in exile. He found it hard to believe such a thing could have happened within their own family. An innocent woman was forever defiled in man's eyes. The seed of hatred and revenge became deeply implanted within Absalom's heart.

David was told of this wickedness. It is recorded that he was very angry, but he didn't punish his son. The hatred intensified in Absalom's heart for Amnon. Day and night he spent his time planning his revenge against his brother. Two years later, the time was right and the coup had been carefully laid. Absalom encouraged friends to party with his brother and to get him drunk, and then murder him. This they did. Again, word was carried to David, now concerning two of his sons: the one dead; the other, an assassin. He wept greatly, grieved not only at the death of his son, but also because Absalom had conspired to do this. But again, no punishment for his son, other than David's refusal to see him, so Absalom continued with a reprobate mind and spirit.

With Amnon out of the way, Absalom's unrepented hatred was now fully transferred to the king. Even though Absalom had been banished from his father's presence, David yearned to see him. Not until he was tricked by the "wise woman of Tekoah," who appealed to the king's known sense of compassion, did David permit his son to return. Absalom falsely honored his father as he: **"came to the king, and bowed himself on his face to the ground before the king: and the king kissed Absalom."** (II Sam. 14,33) On the surface, it looked as if this father-and-son team were working together, but Absalom never repented of the bitterness in his heart; instead, he secretly continued his revenge. Recorded here is the folly of David in sparing his son by indulging him in his wickedness which only deepened Absalom's hard-heartedness.

Outside the palace, the loyal followers of David were taken aside by Absalom who pretended to be of assistance in building his father's kingdom while all the time turning people away by slyly twisting things he said about the king and so: **"Absalom stole the hearts of the men of Israel."** (II Sam. 15:6) Absalom even took advantage of David's desire to have him serve the Lord. He wanted to journey to Hebron to further his efforts to overtake the kingdom, so Absalom went to his father asking him for permission to go to Hebron **"to pay the vow"** which he had made unto the Lord, while his real purpose was to further enhance his following with the king's people. David was overjoyed to hear that Absalom wanted to serve the Lord that not only did he readily give him leave to go but arranged for others to accompany and serve him, all of which worked into Absalom's devious plans.

Absalom sent spies to every part of Israel to incite rebellion against the king until finally the conspiracy became so strong that David was forced to flee for his life. In his hurried evacuation from the palace, David took with him his household, his wives, and children. Ten women, that were concubines, he left behind to keep the house, thinking that their age, sex, and relation to the king would protect them from harm. This, however, was nullified. After David's flight, an advisor to Absalom, Ahithophel, suggested that he should sleep with his father's wives. Ahithophel was the grandfather of Bathsheba. In advising this, he hoped to take revenge upon David for the injury done to his granddaughter. **"So they spread Absalom a tent upon the top of the house; and Absalom went in unto his father's concubines <u>in the sight of all Israel</u>."** (II Sam. 16,22) In this, the Word of God was fulfilled to the letter: that because he defiled Bathsheba, David would have his own wives publicly disgraced.

We next see David preparing to regain control of his kingdom. The decision to stop Absalom had to be made, and this he did. An army was raised, but David was persuaded not to go in person to the battle. His friends expressed their high regard for their king: **"thou art worth 10,000 of us."** David's humble response was **"What seemeth to you best I will do."** His followers probably also knew as did David that his tenderness toward his son would interpose to save the life of Absalom and thus loose the battle. Never was unnatural hatred to a father more strong than in Absalom; nor was ever natural affection to a child more strong in this father - perhaps a similitude designed to picture man's wickedness toward God and God's mercy toward man! David gave charge: **"Deal gently with the young man, even with Absalom, for my sake."** (II Sam. 18:5) He wished above all that his life would be spared.

It is recorded that 20,000 were killed in the battle, but Absalom was spared. As he was returning to his father, escorted by David's men, his mule rode under a tree. A bough caught hold of his head, either by his neck or his hair, we do not know, but there he hung unable to help himself as his mule ran on. The word was spread regarding Absalom's fate. Many wanted to personally kill him, but were afraid to do so because of the well-known affection of the king for his son . . . but there will always be one who will seek revenge. Joab, one of David's leaders threw three darts into Absalom's heart, killing him. Others then came and gave this defector a disgraceful burial by throwing him into a pit.

Returning to David, the men rallied in their great victory, but David at this point was more of a father than a king. His only concern was for the well-being of his son. The news was announced, "Your son is dead." **"And the king was much moved, and went up to the chamber over the gate, and wept: and as he went, thus he said, O my son Absalom, my son, my son Absalom! would God I had died for thee, O Absalom, my son, my son!"**

Even though David repented, the reaping of destruction from rebellion against God's commandments continued to his death. At the end of his life, we read of another of David's sons contriving to illegally take the throne while David was upon his death bed.

Oh, that we may never say again, "David committed adultery and 'got away' with it and this gives me license to commit adultery (and murder). God will simply overlook it if I do it long enough, complicate it through jumbled family trees, and seemingly 'get away' with it!" This is religious folly, accentuated by false application of Biblical history that will bring moral and spiritual ruin. Those who use David's sin as a license to violate a one-flesh covenant should be ready one day to reap an unpleasant harvest: **"For whatsoever a man soweth, that shall he also reap."** (Gal. 6:7) **"Then when lust hath conceived, it bringeth forth sin: and sin, when it is finished, bringeth forth death. <u>Do not err, my beloved brethren.</u>"** (Jas. 1:15,16)

Why should we obey God's commands with or without understanding?

Two things happen regarding God's Word. First, man often doesn't understand why God gives a particular prohibition. God is our Father. We are His children. As is the case with earthly parents and children, man must learn to obey his heavenly Father even when the Word doesn't seem to make sense. As parents, we have years of understanding and experience which cannot be fully explained to our sons and daughters. They are unable to understand the wisdom encompassed in the many decisions parents make. That's why children must be taught to obey without always having an explanation as to why. As adults, this older generation must also follow instructions from employers and peers without always knowing the reasoning behind the requests. Likewise, the proper training of a child would be to respect **righteous** authority (that based upon Biblical principles) without a questioning spirit. This principle must carry over into obedience of God's Word as He, more times than not, gives no answer to many of our questions. We must by faith know that our Father in Heaven knows best and that at some time down the road ". . . **we know that all things work together for good to them that love God, to them who are the called according to his purpose.**" (Rom. 8:28) David probably did not understand the wisdom now written in the first several chapters of Proverbs. **"But whoso committeth adultery with a woman lacketh understanding."** It seems certain that had he comprehended he may not have given in that one time to sleeping with another man's wife. Even though multiple wives were "allowed" by man during this time in history" the taking of another's wife was not. Because man today has the written Word, even more is required of him. God succinctly gives an additional New Testament command: **"And the times of this ignorance God winked at; but now commandeth all men every where to repent."** (Acts 17:30)

Secondly, as also shown through David's personal family tragedies, sin and harvest (sowing and reaping), are often not related because God's timetable is not man's. Judgment may be many years beyond the sowing of seeds of rebellion, saying no to God's word. For some "harvests" of rebellion, the manifestation may go on for many generations. For others, personal harvest comes only after physical death here on earth. Perhaps that was the harvest of King Herod and Herodias who were "permitted" to go on with their reprobate minds - their hearts hardened against the Word of God. God clearly states: **"unto them that are contentious, and do not obey the truth, but obey unrighteousness, indignation and wrath, tribulation and anguish, upon every soul of man that doeth evil."** (Rom. 2:8,9) Only know that what God says, when properly interpreted, always comes to pass. Take a few moments to turn back to pages 80 and 81. Review the five potential reasons given for God's making a permanent record of the account of David's affair with a one-flesh covenant woman.

Let us not leave this subject of sowing and reaping without reviewing the account of a man who <u>chose</u> to continue in obedience to God's most strange command for a period of some 120 years. He probably did ask why in his own mind many times, but he did not stop trusting the Word even when all of the surrounding evidence most likely made him and his family look very foolish.

This man, Noah, lived in a time in which humankind became so wicked and had forsaken his own conscience and the fear of the Lord to such a degree that God was **"grieved at his heart."** Thus in the sixth chapter of Genesis, He announced He would destroy all living things with a flood: **"I will destroy man whom I have created from the face of the earth; both man, and beast, and the creeping thing, and the fowls of the air; for it repenteth me that I have made them."** In all of earth the Lord found only one righteous family, that of Noah: **"Noah was a just man and perfect in his generations, and Noah walked with God."** (Gen. 6:9) Because of his obedient walk with the Lord, God favored Noah and saved his family from the destruction that came unto every other living thing upon this earth. God very specifically detailed an ark which Noah was to construct during the 120-year reprieve He gave to mankind to turn from his wickedness. Man did not repent. Only Noah believed God and prepared.

God very specifically described this ark which Noah was to construct. It was not to be a ship to sail on an extended journey but a vessel made to float. Specific instructions for the ark included the type of wood, exact dimensions, the number of stories, and how the interior space was to be allocated. Housed in this ark were to be Noah and his one-flesh mate, their three sons and their covenant wives, food and water, and animals to "replenish the earth." In his obedience to God's Word, **"Thus did Noah; according to all that God commanded him, so did he."** The Lord showed through this historical example that man and God are a team and that none can be saved except by following God's plan for salvation. We can't do it without God, <u>and</u> He doesn't do it without us.

For some 120 years, Noah continued in what neighbors might have jeered, "Noah's folly":

> Hey, Noah, what's the rain report today? (It, until the time of the flood, had never rained upon the earth even though there were bodies of water.) Noah, it's only been 100 years since God said we were going to have a flood. Why in the world are you still building that ridiculous boat?

Every blow of the hammer and stroke of the ax could have been a call to repentance for this wicked generation. They, too, could have prepared an ark "to the saving of their families," but disbelief of God's Word was their free-will choice. They could accept or reject the message.

The rains did come - for 40 days and nights, preceded by a final seven-day forewarning: **"And the Lord said unto Noah Come thou and all thy house into the ark; for thee have I seen righteous before me in this generation . . . For yet seven days, and I will cause it to rain upon the earth forty days and forty nights; and every living substance that I have made will I destroy from off the earth."** (Gen. 7:1-4) God himself closed the door of the ark after only Noah, his family, and the animals were safely inside.

As mentioned earlier, man often does not understand why certain things happen in his life nor does he comprehend the reasoning behind many of God's commands. Perhaps during Noah's 120 years of obedient faith he, too, had some moments of doubt. Centuries later, we are told what perhaps Noah "knew in his heart" as he persevered in obeying God as he **"moved with fear, prepared an ark"** . . . and the reason for this, the reward which any parent might covet who knows the blessing of salvation . . . **"to the saving of his house."**! (Heb. 11:7) This family through Noah's steadfastness and righteous living were chosen by God . . . as is every man. Many, however do not choose to follow God. The latter, it is said, will be destroyed.

In Noah's day, the entire civilization became so wicked that God's righteous judgment "gave" them over to the consequence of their vile lifestyles - destruction. They had repeatedly violated Divine laws. Everyone except for

Noah and his family were lost in the waters of the flood. With the Pharoah, God sent his servant Moses ten times to bring Truth, but each time the king rebelled until his heart was so hardened that he was killed along with thousands of his followers by drowning in the Red Sea. Saul and David both answered the call to serve the Lord. Both chose rebellion, but Saul refused to repent. He tried to cover his sin by pretense of worship and the offering of sacrifices. He died in torment. David repented of his sins against God and was spared but from that time until his death he saw only destruction within his family. Noah waited and waited in obedience and faith and . . . one day saw the reason for God's strange command.

Noah is only one of many listed in the eleventh chapter of Hebrews, called the faith chapter. This "hall of fame" includes not only Noah who **"by faith being warned of God of things not seen as yet moved with fear, prepared an ark,"** but many others. Some of those listed also saw their prayers answered; however, many did not. They died waiting; others **"had trial of cruel mockings and scourgings . . . imprisonment, were stoned, were sawn asunder, were slain with the sword."** But still they believed, and it is recorded that they received a good report.

Many mock God's Word. Others believe it's just a history book. Some feel that it's not applicable today. Each person has that choice of interpretation. The doubter should know, however, that over 300 prophesies of the Old Testament regarding the birth, death, and resurrection of Christ have been accurately fulfilled centuries after the foretelling. Over 90 percent of the original manuscripts of the Bible has been found on pottery and other documents and supported by archaeological finds.

Man with all of his knowledge still searches to uncover truth behind mysteries which God has created. Recorded in the book of Job, one of the oldest texts of the Bible, is written a conversation between Job and God. In Chapters 37 and 38 are surveyed issue after issue that man with all of his wisdom even today cannot answer. We are not here to understand every aspect of life but to let the Father teach us how to live according to Biblical principles. We each need to learn from God that we may leave this earth ready to enjoy an eternity reaping righteousness rather than spending infinity reaping torment for rebellious lifestyles: **"And if thy eye offend thee, pluck it out: it is better for thee to enter into the kingdom of God with one eye, than having two eyes to be cast into hell fire: Where their worm dieth not and the fire is not quenched."** (Mark 9:47,48)

CHAPTER 7
WHAT WAS HOSEA'S HEARTBREAK?

"Go get your adulterous wife. Bring her back home. Pay the ransom to buy her back from her illicit partners."

Who would make what seems like such a ridiculous command? Only someone who understands agape love would so suggest. This command was made by God to Hosea, a man who lived sometime around 750 B.C. Hosea didn't "volunteer" for his prophetic and personal ministry; the Lord called him. The Lord commands everyone to **"Go ye therefore into all the world and preach the gospel."** We each decide whether to obey or rebel. Hosea had the free-will choice to accept or reject the work placed before him. He submitted to the call.

Instead of following Hosea's pattern of obedience, many do as did Jonah, another Old Testament prophet, regarding the "works of the Spirit": they run from God's directive **"Now the word of the Lord came unto Jonah, the son of Amittai, saying, Arise, go to Nineveh, that great city, and cry against it; for their wickedness is come up before me."** Jonah was asked to tell one of the most vile, corrupt nations in the world that they were going to be destroyed unless they changed their lifestyles. Nineveh was the center of the Assyrian monarchy, a huge city some 48 miles in diameter, immensely wealthy, yet a corrupt, heathen city. Jonah's call was to witness against its great wickedness, a most frightening directive. What was his response?

"But Jonah rose up <u>to flee</u> unto Tarshish <u>from the presence of the Lord</u>, and went down to Joppa; and he found a ship going to Tarshish: so he paid the fare thereof, and went down into it, to go with them unto Tarshish <u>from the presence of the Lord</u>." Here we see a man who wasn't turning from the Lord because of sins of the flesh as we normally associate but because of his fear of the calling upon his life. Jonah* eventually turned from this dishonoring of the Lord and did as he was called, but he did meet with extensive personal afflictions in the interim.

It is indeed difficult to "swim against the tide" which is what is required if messages from the Bible are to be preached unto the world. In this chapter we will be looking at two men who determined from the time that the "Word came unto them" to do as the Lord commanded. These two prophets were Hosea and Jeremiah. Both of these men of God brought messages which contained parallel teachings about the marriage-covenant. Hosea's experience was centered around his personal family heartache; Jeremiah's message was told through his torment and suffering from the hands of the very people he tried to save from destruction. Both accounts included a symbolic representation of God's lifetime covenant to a nation that committed spiritual adultery and many other immoral sins against the covenant between it and God. Clearly shown through both prophets is that man's sin does not nullify a covenant with God.

Hosea and Jeremiah's "audience" differed from Jonah's in that the people to whom they pleaded were God's chosen people; those who had the Word, read it, studied it, but were rebelling against it.

What was the Lord's message through the prophet Hosea?

With Hosea, in addition to being commanded to tell people that their lifestyles were an abomination, he was to suffer the personal pain and humiliation of loving an unfaithful wife. His agape love to an adulterous mate was a message unto people of all ages. It symbolized the pain

---

*Jonah signifies a dove. The dove, throughout the New Testament, symbolizes the Holy Spirit descending from heaven unto His beloved people.

that they inflict upon the Holy Spirit when they reject the saving grace made available to them by the person of Jesus Christ. He was stripped, beaten, humiliated, and nailed to a cross willingly . . . to suffer. God gave **"his only begotten Son, that whosoever believeth in him should not perish, but have everlasting life."** (John 3:16) God made a covenant with Israel, but it applied to peoples of all ages - that salvation is a gift from the Lord for <u>repentant</u> people everywhere. This promise was made in the context of a marriage-covenant. It was made to a nation that broke it. In this "agreement" God called himself a husband to the Jewish nation, setting the standard for the husband over a household. The marriage-covenant between Him and them, the people broke by idolatry - spiritual adultery. They turned from Him to other gods - divorced Him - committed treachery. (Recall in Chapter Four that the men who turned from their covenant wives and married others were quoted as dealing treacherously, but even so God still considered the rebellious mates in covenant with **"the wife of thy youth . . . the wife of thy covenant."**) (Mal. 2:14)

We see in both the Old and New Testaments God using the marriage-covenant as an analogy to picture individuals and nations in right and wrong relationships with each other and with Him. Ephesians Five is an example of marriage being used as the symbolic relationship of Christ and the church - His people: **"Wives, submit yourselves unto your <u>own husbands</u>, as unto the Lord. For the husband is head of the wife, <u>even as Christ is the head of the church</u> . . . Husbands, love your wives even <u>as Christ also loved the church</u>, <u>and</u> <u>gave</u> <u>himself</u> <u>for</u> <u>it</u>."**

Recorded in the book of Hosea are two parallel historically documented events involving adultery: the first, that of a spouse; the second, that of a nation. Each of these gives us a picture of anguish, hurt, disappointment . . . pain worse than that of the physical death of a loved one - spurned love against a background of agape love. Hosea, as a part of God's "call" was to suffer the pain and humiliation of loving an unfaithful wife as well as to petition his fellow countrymen to turn from their apostasy from the Lord.

After their marriage and the birth of three children, Hosea's wife, Gomer, left him and went to live with other men. Certainly, many would say that Hosea had "Scriptural" reason to divorce Gomer - that she had broken the marriage-covenant. From previous chapters of this text, we know this to be false doctrine. Under Old Testament Jewish customs, this prophet could have claimed Deuteronomy 24:4, had her stoned to death, or maybe even given a bill of divorcement - if adultery were not apparent. God, however, abates all of these man-made allowances and, as we will see, specifically shows His disapproval of man's practice of applying Deuteronomy 24:4 to a marriage-covenant.

The Lord told Hosea to go and get his wife and bring her back home. He was to love her even though she "loved adultery." God even tells Hosea how to love his wife - with agape love - the love of the Lord: **"Then said the Lord unto me, Go yet love a woman beloved of her friends, yet an adulteress, according to the love of the Lord toward the children of Israel, who look to other gods and love flagons of wine."** (Hosea 3:1)

Prior to this, Hosea had asked his children to plead with their mother to stop her harlotry, to quit giving herself to other men. Because of Gomer's behavior, she and Hosea were not living as husband and wife, even though they were in God's eyes still one flesh: **"Plead with your mother, plead: for she is not my wife, neither am I her husband: let her therefore put away her whoredoms out of her sight, and her adulteries from between her breasts; Lest I strip her naked, and set her as in the day that she was born . . . For their mother hath played the harlot; she that conceived them hath done shamefully: for she said, I will go after my lovers."** (Hosea 2:2-5)

Intricately interwoven with Hosea's personal family tragedy is God's pleading through Hosea with the children of Israel to return to Him. He warns them of forthcoming destruction if they do not stop their worship of false gods. Even in their turning from Him to sin, God lets the people know that the covenant still stands. The Lord lists Israel's sins in Chapter Four: **"Hear the word of the Lord, ye children of Israel: for the Lord hath a** controversy with the inhabitants of the land . . . By **swearing**, and **lying**, and **killing**, and **stealing**, and **committing adultery** . . ."

We have seen previously in this text that part of God's judgment, the consequence of rejecting Divine law, is the hardening of the heart where man's conscience is seared and he no longer is bothered by the transgressions against God's Word. In this state man feels that he has God's approval and is "getting away" with sin. God, after many warnings through several prophets, begins His judgment on the nation of Israel: "I **will not punish** your daughters when they commit whoredoms, nor your spouses when they commit adultery: for themselves are separated with whores, and they sacrifice with harlots: therefore the people that doth not understand **shall fall**." (Hosea 4:14)

Just prior to this warning from the mouth of Hosea, the Lord gave this message: "**My people are destroyed for lack of knowledge: because thou hast rejected knowledge, I will also reject thee.**" In His judgment against them the Lord foretells through Hosea that the people will look for Him but won't find Him because they have "divorced" themselves from Him; i.e., dealt treacherously: "**They shall go with their flocks and with their herds to seek the Lord; but they shall not find him; he hath withdrawn himself from them. They have dealt treacherously against the Lord.**" (Hosea 5:7) The chastisement continues in Chapter Six: "**But they like men have transgressed the covenant: they have dealt treacherously against me.**" Within His warning, the Lord includes those in the ministry who give approval to man remaining in sin: "**the company of priests murder in the way of consent.**" The leaders of the church by approving of the sin that man commits become a part of the destruction of man "by way of consent."

God looks at the heart from which should flow the fruit of the spirit. He measures that against the lust (works) of the flesh, man's lifestyle. (Gal. 5:19-23) He continues: "**And they consider not in their hearts that I remember all their wickedness . . . They are all adulterers . . . They do not return to the Lord, their God, nor seek him for all this.**" Even though the Lord pleads repeatedly with His people, they refuse to turn from sin. His sad response through Hosea is: "**Woe unto them! for they have fled from me: destruction unto them! because they have transgressed against me: though I have redeemed them, yet they have spoken lies against me. And they have not cried unto me with their heart, when they howled upon their beds.**" Here we see recorded that man cries because of perhaps some hardships beginning to be reaped from sin, but man's heart has not changed - he still continues in what God calls sin: "**Though I have bound and strengthened their arms, yet do they imagine mischief against me. They return, but not to the most high . . . Ye have plowed wickedness, ye have reaped iniquity; ye have eaten the fruit of lies . . . Therefore shall a tumult arise among thy people, and all thy fortresses shall be spoiled.**" (Hosea 10:13,14)

The book of Hosea ends with a final plea that was not heeded by the people. They were, except for a small believing remnant, destroyed: "**O Israel, return unto the Lord thy God; for thou hast fallen by thine iniquity.**" Again expressed is the agape love that will forever be there . . . for the returning man, woman, child, spouse: "**I will heal their backsliding, I will love them freely: for mine anger is turned away from him . . . the ways of the Lord are right, and the just shall walk in them; but the transgressors shall fall therein.**" (Hosea 14: 4,9)

The Lord clearly states the resulting benefit of His grace expressed through accepted agape love. This is salvation, but it is two-sided. Salvation is available _if_ man turns from sin. Then He will heal the hurts, love them freely, turn from them His anger. The same analogy is meant to be extended to a one-flesh mate as is recorded through the life of Hosea with God's command to this prophet regarding Gomer's adulterous lifestyle: "**love . . . according to the love of the Lord toward the children of Israel, who look to other gods, and love flagons of wine.**" (Hosea 3:1) In the New Testament, the command is the same: "**Husbands, love your wives, even as Christ also loved the church, and gave himself for it.**" (Eph. 5:25)

God made an everlasting covenant with the nation of Israel. It still stands today. The people broke the "vows"

. . . by worshipping other gods . . . by committing adultery . . . by lying; but the covenant still stood. They were still responsible to God and without returning to the covenant they made with God, they would die and face eternal torment.

What was the Lord's message through the prophet Jeremiah?

Jeremiah foretold of the destruction of his beloved nation. He, too, cried out to the people to repent. Jeremiah was called the weeping prophet. He was a man of sorrows and knew well grief in that he was a suffering man of God who was persecuted by his own countrymen - those he tried to save from destruction. The book of Jeremiah is important not only because it is the same message to the rebellious Israelites but also because within Jeremiah's calling is the specific setting aside of many of the established Jewish customs. One of these we examined earlier in this text, the prohibition forbidding a spouse to return to a mate once he had left her. God dispels the aforementioned not only in the book of Jeremiah but in many other chapters in the Old Testament through His examples of being forever committed regardless of the transgression of His covenant people. He waits for the turning from sin - which may or may not happen. In the New Testament Scriptures, we clearly noted the teachings regarding the permanence of the one-flesh marriage-covenant which is only nullified by the death of one of the spouses.

To review, Deuteronomy 24:4 says: "**Her former husband, which sent her away, may not take her again to be his wife, after that she is defiled.**" This Scripture is misapplied today when a spouse leaves a covenant mate and takes an illicit partner as a spouse. This Scripture is then "used" to say that the one-flesh mates cannot return to each other. We do not, however, find these same people "abiding" by the many other Jewish laws and customs. Refer again to some of the Old Testament prohibitions that man today chooses not to follow or to make mention of: "**When a man hath taken a new wife, he shall not go out to war, neither shall he be** charged with any business: but he shall be free at home <u>one year</u>." (Deu. 24:5) We also know that under Jewish law, contained in these same teachings were the directives that adulterers and adulteresses were to be stoned to death. Additionally recall the prohibition against the wearing of a garment that was made of more than one fiber: **"neither shall a garment mingled of linen and woollen come upon thee."** (Lev. 19:19) Children who disobeyed their parents were, (according to the "law/custom") also to be stoned to death! Blood sacrifices of animals were regularly required by everyone as an atonement for sin.

Today, we don't follow any of the above. If we are saved, we know that our atonement for sin is Jesus Christ and that with sin, we are to repent and forgive. With children, we are to bring them up in the fear and admonition of the Lord by diligently teaching them the Word of God and providing a Godly example for them to duplicate.

In Chapter Three of Jeremiah's message, the Lord, through this prophet, clearly dispels wrong teachings about Deuteronomy 24:4. We are given the picture of a rebellious nation which is portrayed as an adulterous wife. This nation, Israel, is "a spouse" who has **"played the harlot with many lovers . . . thou hast polluted the land with thy whoredoms and with thy wickedness . . . Hast thou seen that which backsliding Israel hath done? She is gone up upon every high mountain and under every green tree, and there hath played the harlot."** The "normal" counsel to this type of behavior from a spouse would be to leave him/her, to file for a divorce. "Why would you want anyone back who has done such a thing?" Let's study God's example given for our instruction. **"And I said <u>after she had done all these things</u>, Turn thou unto me . . . Return, thou backsliding Israel, saith the Lord; and I will not cause mine anger to fall upon you: for I am merciful, saith the Lord . . . Only <u>acknowledge thine iniquity</u>, that thou hast transgressed against the Lord . . . <u>Turn</u>, O backsliding children, saith the Lord; for <u>I am married unto you</u>."** (Jer. 3:7-14) Sin does not annul a covenant made between man and God, whether it be murder, prostitution, adultery, lying, or cheating.

God, in this chapter, also makes it very clear that it

was man, not He who put in place the Deuteronomy 24 permission to deal with man's hard-heartedness, just as were the "bill of divorcement" and the stoning for sexual sins. (Man today strongly favors the "bill of divorcement" but has rejected the practice of stoning adulterers and adulteresses!) Turn again to Jeremiah Three but this time to verse one: "**They say, If a man put away his wife, and she go from him, and become another man's, shall he return unto her again? shall not that land be greatly polluted?**" But . . . the Lord tells the people that they have done the same thing to Him. He does not, however, tell them that they cannot repent, be forgiven, and come back into fellowship with Him: "**But thou has played the harlot with many lovers; yet return again unto me, saith the Lord . . . Turn, O backsliding children . . . for I am married unto you.**" Though a **treacherous wife, yet a wife, for I am married to you:** "**Because the Lord hath been witness between thee and the wife of thy youth, against whom thou hast dealt treacherously: yet is she thy companion, and thy wife of thy covenant. And did he not make one?**" (Mal. 2:14,15)

"**Surely as a wife treacherously departeth from her husband, so have ye dealt treacherously with me, O house of Israel, said the Lord. Return, ye backsliding children and I will heal your backslidings.**" (Jer. 3:20-22) Again, the Lord speaks of divorce (treachery), of adultery, of all sin, and the fact that agape love waits for repentance, for the turning from sin, for the backslider to return to the commandments of the Lord. "**But whoso keepeth his word, in him verily is the love of God perfected: hereby know we that we are in him. He that saith he abideth in him ought himself also so to walk, even as he walked.**" (I John 2:5,6)

In Chapter Four, the pleading continues: "**If thou wilt return, O Israel, said the Lord, return unto me: and if thou wilt put away thine abominations out of my sight . . .**" (Jer. 4:1) Sin must be put away out of the heart or it is not put away from the Lord. There can be no more desire for what God calls sin.

To rid oneself of the desire for sin and to have the grace to give agape love toward a mate, a child, a friend, or an enemy, one must turn to the Lord for help. Hypnotism, seances, affairs, drugs, psychiatrists are only Band-aids. They will not cure. They will not bring about a relationship with the Lord. Only strength and grace from the Lord can break a hold on sin and provide the "ointment" for pain dispersed because of rebellion. The plea of the Lord goes throughout our land: **"<u>Today</u> if ye will hear his voice,** (His voice meaning what the Word says) **<u>harden not your hearts as in the provocation</u> . . . when your fathers tempted me, proved me, and saw my works forty years. Wherefore I was grieved with that generation and said, They do always err in their heart; and they have not known my ways. So I sware in my wrath, They shall not enter into my rest."** (Heb. 3:8-11)

Some may say, "but the Word says: **'When thou vowest a vow unto God, defer not to pay it . . . neither say thou before the angel, that it was an error: wherefore should God be angry at thy voice, and destroy the work of thine hands?'** (Ecc. 5:4,6) When I married another spouse, I made another vow that I must now keep. Won't God forgive me for the first marriage?" There is nothing to forgive regarding your original one-flesh covenant. That was not and is not the sin. The problem is an illegal vow that was made in rebellion to God's Divine law regarding marriage. No man can by a vow make that lawful which God says is unlawful. Recall in Chapter Five that King Herod made a "vow" to Salome, **"Ask of me whatsoever thou wilt, and I will give it thee. And he sware unto her, Whatsoever thou shalt ask of me, I will give it thee, unto the half of my kingdom."** When Salome returned with the request that her mother had given her - the head of John the Baptist - King Herod could have refused. God would not have held him to such an ungodly, vile revengeful vow.

Return again to the book of Jeremiah. In Chapter Four, we find Jeremiah pleading with the people to stop their sacrificing to idols and making vows which were ungodly. He told them that God would destroy them for such rebellion. The Jews answered Jeremiah: **"As for the word that thou hast spoken unto us in the name of the Lord, <u>we will not hearken</u> unto thee. But we will certainly do whatsoever thing goeth forth out of our own mouth . . ."** (Verses 16,17) Through

Jeremiah the Lord responded: "**Because ye have burned incense, and because ye have sinned against the Lord, and have not obeyed the voice of the Lord, nor walked in his law, nor in his statutes, nor in his testimonies; therefore this evil is happened unto you, as at this day . . . Ye and your wives have both spoken with your mouths, and fulfilled with your hand, saying, We will surely <u>perform our vows that we have vowed</u> . . . ye will surely accomplish your vows, and surely perform your vows.**" The people were set on carrying out vows that were an abomination to the Lord. They chose to "sow" destruction and now they would "reap" the <u>wages</u> of disobedience: "**Therefore hear ye the word of the Lord, all Judah that dwell in the land of Egypt; Behold, I have sworn by my great name, saith the Lord, that my name shall no more be named in the mouth of any man of Judah . . . I will watch over them for evil, and not for good: and all the men of Judah that are in the land of Egypt shall be consumed by the sword and by the famine, until there be an end of them . . . I will punish you in this place, that ye may know that my words shall surely stand against you for evil.**" (Jer. 44:26-29) Yes, the people "got away" with sin - for awhile, but their <u>wages</u> were death and destruction. Sinners in their deception say that they shall have peace in their rebellious lifestyles; God says they will have no peace.

They that sow in tears shall reap in joy. He that goeth forth and weepeth <u>bearing precious seed</u>, shall doubtless come again with rejoicing, bringing his sheaves with him." (Psa. 126:6) Those who suffer for the sake of the Truth of the Word may have much despair as did the prophets of old. They will share in the calamities of human life and often have even a greater share of them than others but even so, their weeping must not hinder their sowing of Divine seeds. When we suffer ill we must still be doing well. The Lord's prophets sustained much unwarranted abuse, but they stored up treasures in Heaven. Even Job who lost home, family, friends, and wealth, and suffered intense physical and mental pain, at the end of his life was greatly blessed: "**So the Lord blessed the latter end of Job more than his beginning: for he had fourteen thousand**

sheep, and six thousand camels, and a thousand yoke of oxen, and a thousand she asses. He had also seven sons and three daughters . . . after this lived Job a hundred and forty years, and saw his sons, and his sons' sons, even four generations."** (Job 42:12-16) In contrast, not all receive rewards and answers to prayer on this earth: **"and others were tortured . . . And others had trial of cruel mockings and scourgings."** (Heb. 11:35,36) . . . and Jesus Christ was nailed to a cross!

"Return unto the Lord with all your hearts"
(I Sam. 7:3)

EPILOGUE

A word of caution must be appended to the love story of Hosea and Gomer. Those who have mates who have left the home are not by this example encouraged to run out and attempt to physically bring their mates home. If there has been a breaking of a relationship between husband and wife, there will most likely be accompanying feelings of extreme hatred, jealousy, anger, resentment. Those who have mates who have threatened their one-flesh spouse with physical harm or have actually carried out such acts should not be "tempted" to do so again.

Each person must face and deal with his/her situation as the Lord leads - <u>but</u> according to Scriptural principles. We do not know the Lord's timetable. With Hosea, it appears that his ministry lasted some forty years. It is not recorded how many years he waited before the Lord commanded him to go and get Gomer.

If a mate is not willing to talk and to try to work things out, the remaining spouse must <u>wait</u> . . . and hold on to the Lord for the strength to do so.

> "But
> they that wait upon the Lord
> shall renew their strength;
> they shall mount up with wings as eagles;
> they shall run, and not be weary;
> and they shall walk and not faint."
> (Isa. 40:31)

CHAPTER 8
WHAT DOES GOD HAVE TO SAY TO THE CHURCHES?

"For the time is come that judgment
must begin at the house of God."
I Peter 4:17

"Woe unto them that call evil good, and good evil;
that put darkness for light, and light for darkness;
that put bitter for sweet, and sweet for bitter!"
Isaiah 5:20

"Woe be unto the pastors that
destroy and scatter the sheep of my pasture!"
Jeremiah 23:1

Many people ask the question: "What is wrong with today's youth?" Why is there so much crime in America? It is true that not a day passes that we don't hear or read about crime in our nation, about the drug problem, about the increasing crime rate, about juvenile delinquency, about the breakdown of the family. We cannot build prisons fast enough to house those who refuse to conform to society's standards. Our mental institutions, reform schools, and other correctional and remedial institutions are bursting at the seams. The news media report that our nation's leaders are considering a contract for $48 million a year to buy opium from Khun Sa, one of the world's most-wanted outlaws and criminals. In his poppy fields in Burma, he produces the largest amount of drugs used in our country. The rationale behind the government's consideration of a "deal" with this man is that our leaders would destroy the opium and thus cut down on our problem here. Khun Sa, however, is not the source of the problem; the heart of man is. Man is deceived into thinking that you can put a Band-aid on a badly infected area and that what is underneath will heal.

Our government conducts multimillion-dollar surveys and directs studies and hearings to prove what we already know about AIDS, juvenile delinquency, and pornography. No one will face the problem: a nation which has turned away from God, a nation which encourages the breakdown of the family unit, church leadership which teaches heresy and preaches sermons to "tickle" man's ears. We see not only ordinary citizens but also those in the ministry falling prey to sexual lust and materialistic desires.

Mentioned earlier in this text was the fact that over fifty percent of the marriages in America end up in a divorce proceeding. Since 1970 our nation has experienced the destruction of over a million families every year. What is the cause of this national tragedy? In one of its most comprehensive studies on the topic of broken families, the United States government in 1983 conducted a series of hearings called <u>Oversight on the Breakdown of the Traditional Family Unit, Focusing on the Causes and Implications for Society and the Role of Government in Helping Prevent The Breakup of Families</u>. This particular study was done under the direction of U.S. Senator Jeremiah Denton (R.AL). Experts from many differing fields gave testimony, polls were taken, and data statistically analyzed. The results were published in two volumes by our government. Comments are shared below from two of the witnesses; the first, Midge Decter, executive director, Committee for the Free World; second, Dr. Amitai Etzioni, Director, Center for Policy Research at George Washington University. (Emphasis is added by underlining.)

> For a generation now, millions upon millions of Americans - I will not say all - have been engaging in <u>child sacrifice</u>. Less bloodily, perhaps, but no less obediently than certain ancient groups of idol worshipers, we have been offering up our children on the altar of a pitiless god. (See II Kings 3:27;17:17.) Nor do

I mean this as a flowery metaphor. In our case, the idol to whom we have sacrificed our young is not made of wood or gold, but of an idea. This idea, very crudely put, is that we are living in an altogether new world with not yet fully understood new moral rules. As inhabitants of this supposedly newly ordered world, we tell ourselves we have no right to cling to or impose on others outmoded standards of behavior. On the contrary, everyone has a right, even an obligation, to make up his own rules - and with these rules, to make up his own preferred mode of living . . . And <u>we have, as I said, literally sacrificed our children to it</u>. One thing about which we seem to have achieved near-universal agreement is that something is going wrong with the constitution of our private lives.

Miss Decker, the speaker, continues by mentioning our drug and alcohol problems and the unsuccessful efforts to solve them. She questions the rationale for divorce.

And, of course, there are all those divorces, all those lonely and self-seeking men and women, hopping from marriage to marriage in search of they know not what, all those children abandoned by their fathers, and even, nowadays abandoned by their mothers . . . How is it that people blessed by God with better health, longer lives, greater comfort, and personal freedom and economic well-being than any previous people in human history should give so much evidence of deep trouble?

Continuing, Miss Decker talks about moral irresponsibility and that none of the authorities in the lives of children will tell them what they need to know:

. . . that life is real and weighty and consequential; that it requires discipline and courage and the assumption of responsibility for oneself and others . . . <u>We are permitting ourselves to become a society that punishes the virtuous. That punishment is every day being incorporated into the laws of the land, written and unwritten</u> . . . In attempting to erase its uniqueness as an institution, we remove from the family the community affirmation that is the absolutely essential ingredient to its strength as an institution . . . Indeed, by <u>turning the family into a merely voluntary, optional relationship</u>, we have ironically increased its capacity to make its members unhappy. Thus our divorce rate.

To be a parent is to discover, sometimes with considerable surprise, at first, that there are lives more valuable to one than one's own. To be a child of parents is to incorporate into one's being the knowledge that human life, as opposed to animal existence, is a system of mutual obligations and dependencies.

To get beyond self is the only possibility for happiness; to understand obligation is the only possibility for genuine individual freedom. That may, as little children are wont to say, be 'no fair,' but it is the truth. Thus, the family to me . . . is a mother and a father <u>and their children</u>.

In a letter to Senator Denton, Miss Decter wrote: "But if Capitol Hill could still, as it once was, be a place shocked by adultery, pederasty, and other sins - if such things at least still cost one something in the highest tribunal of the land - it would make an enormous difference to our entire public tone." (1:1-8)

Dr. Etzioni reminded the Senate subcommittee that no society has ever survived without the family as the core unit of society and discussed the tragic effects on the children:

As we talk now about no-fault divorce which has a legal meaning, but as a different sociological signal, much more of <u>our culture has gone in the direction of promoting</u> the <u>antifamily forces</u> . . . Let me say first of all that in all my professional and personal experience I have never seen a single child, not one, who did not suffer, in one way or another, psychically or psychosomatically, to one degree or another, from divorce . . . We dare not allow the family to collapse. There never was a society throughout all of history - and many variations society exhibited - without a family as the central unit for launching the education of children, for character formation, and as the moral agent of society." (2:21-27)

Dr. Etzioni clearly stated that "mail-order divorce" should be prohibited, that procedure being made available through the No-fault Divorce statute. As Dr. Etzioni noted, we have seen that subsequent to the passage of the "Uniform Marriage and Divorce Act" in 1970, the rapid "progress" being made in incorporating into each of the statutes of our fifty states the principles needed to promote the breakdown of the family unit in America. And . . . we are reaping nationwide destruction because of it.

Why must judgment start at the house of the Lord?

Man's morality will be dictated by his theology. America's theology is surely one of rebellion against God's Word, the Bible. He is saying, "I don't believe it is Truth." God tells us that **"judgment must start <u>at the house of the Lord</u>"** - the church: the body of believers calling themselves Christians. Second Peter and Jude are two books which warn against false teachers and the punishment awaiting them as well as warnings and pleadings for those <u>saved</u> and <u>unsaved</u> not to fall prey to false teachings. God will not spare anyone who determines to turn from Him, or who refuses to turn to Him, or who leads His people astray - who does not <u>repent</u> with "Godly sorrow." (II Cor. 7:10) Those in or out of the church will reap consequences of reprobate lifestyles.

"I will therefore put you in remembrance, though ye once knew this, how that the Lord, <u>having saved</u> the people out of the land of Egypt, <u>afterward</u> destroyed them <u>that believed not</u>." (Jude 5)

"And the angels which kept not their first estate . . . he hath reserved in everlasting chains under darkness unto the judgment of the great day." (Jude 6)

"Even as Sodom and Gomorrah, and the cities about them in like manner, giving themselves over to fornication, and going after strange flesh, are set forth <u>for an example</u>, suffering the vengeance of <u>eternal fire</u>." (Jude 7)

"But whoso offend one of these little ones which believe in me, it were better for him that a millstone were hanged about his neck, and that he were drowned in the depth of the sea." (Matt. 18:6)

"Woe be unto the pastors that destroy and scatter the sheep of my pasture! saith the Lord." (Jer. 23:1)

"Woe unto them! for they have gone in the error of Balaam for reward, and perished in the gainsaying of Korah." "Having eyes full of adultery, and that <u>cannot cease from sin</u>; beguiling unstable souls: a heart they have exercised with covetous practices; cursed children: Which have <u>forsaken</u> the right way, and are gone astray, following the way of Balaam the son of Bosor, <u>who loved the</u> <u>wages</u> <u>of unrighteousness</u>." (II Pet. 2:14,15)

In Chapters 22 to 25 of Numbers is the account of a prophet once used mightily of God. He, however, was lured by the lust for money and turned Truth into error. He led the nation of Israel into sinful relationships with Moabite and Midianite women. Balaam, along with 24,000 Israelites perished because of these sinful acts. This former prophet's name, instead of being identified with righteousness, became a synonym for one who becomes a stumbling block and leads others into sexual perversions. (See also Rev. 2:14.)

Shepherds and elders, leadership in the churches, are to be examples to those who hear their teachings and see their lifestyles. They are to **"Feed the flock of God which is among you . . . not for filthy lucre, but of a ready mind . . . <u>being ensamples</u> to the flock."** (I Pet. 5:1-4) Those in leadership are to preach the Truth as given in the Scriptures and to direct "their flocks" as the Word of God prescribes through Biblical instruction and personal examples.

Church people blame the government and non-Christians for the crime and perversion running rampant in America. The church, however, perhaps without realizing it, has played a major role in the "harvest" of a nation that is now openly rejecting the Bible and the godly principles established by the author of that book. As mentioned above, man mocks the Bible not only by rejecting the Truths in it but by teaching doctrines that are not found in the Word of God. When Biblical Truth is rejected, God is rejected. This is especially true in the area of the permanence of the institution of marriage. Church members have conformed their minds to the world's standard of marriage rather than being transformed by the renewing of their minds to the Truths in the word . . . that they may <u>prove</u> what is that good, and acceptable, and perfect will of God regarding marriage: **"And be not conformed to this world: but be ye transformed by the renewing of your mind, that ye may prove what is that good, and acceptable, and perfect, will of God."** (Rom. 12:2)

Born-again, spirit-filled Christians will advise divorced people to marry another spouse - especially if the mate has been what they consider a "scoundrel" or if "sufficient" time has elapsed since the unfaithful mate left the home - rather than encouraging the abandoned mate to abide by what the Scriptures and the marriage-covenant and vows clearly and distinctly command. Few church members quote Scriptures like **"whosoever divorces his wife and marrieth another committeth adultery** and the many others discussed in earlier chapters of this text. Instead, emphasis is placed upon the "for worse" aspects of a marriage and the world's way of dealing with unfaithfulness - get on with your life: find another spouse. Sad but true is the fact that the divorce rate of those attending church in America is quickly catching up with those who do not attend. How has this abomination happened?

To get a clearer picture, we will first explore specific warnings and guidelines given in the Bible relating to church leadership and the messages God directs its leaders to teach. This will be contrasted with the changing doctrines in major church denominations as well as small fellowships regarding the permanence of the institution of marriage. With such an overview, perhaps the reader will be able to understand how the changing "nature" of the church has been mirrored by man in his twisted misunderstandings of what is good and what is evil and thus the moral decadence of our nation.

In Chapter Two of this text, the definition of love was discussed. It was stated that the failure of love in a marriage to last is related to the fact that man does not know God. God is love. This principle was likewise applied to marriage. In a like manner, man, in his lack of understanding God, does not comprehend the examples He has left for us to imitate within the confines of a commitment to a life-time marriage-covenant. As we saw in Chapter Seven, God's continuing covenant with His people has never been nullified by sin. This binding covenant relationship is to be an example for man to duplicate in marriage. Man, however, has failed to teach each succeeding generation Biblical Truth until today divorce and second marriages have falsely become "Biblical Truth." We have failed to follow an Old Testament command and are reaping horrible consequences: **"fear the Lord, thy God, to keep all his statutes and his commandments . . . and these words, which I command thee this day, shall be in thine heart: And thou shalt teach them <u>diligently</u> unto thy children, and shalt talk of them when thou sittest in thine house, and when thou** walkest by the way, and when thou liest down, and when thou risest up." (Deu. 6:2,6,7)

Review again the commands given in Romans 12:2. We are not to be conformed to this world. We are to be transformed to know the good, acceptable, and perfect will of God by renewing our mind with what the Scriptures command. Minds taught by the "soaps" on television, and by the literature on the newsstands, will only eventually bring total destruction to our nation. Society "cannot" follow God's standards for His institution of marriage because Biblical Truths have been changed into lies as man has been beguiled ever so gradually by the same technique as was used with Eve in the garden of Eden: **"Ye shall not surely die . . ."** (Gen. 3:4)

Warnings are posted throughout the Scriptures for those who are saved to beware lest they, too, fall. In the third chapter of Hebrews is the example of the multitudes that the Lord saved out of Egypt, <u>but</u> they hardened their hearts, and God, after repeatedly giving them opportunities to repent stated: **"So I sware in my wrath, They shall not enter into my rest. Take heed, <u>brethren</u>, lest there be in any of you an evil heart of unbelief, in <u>departing</u> from the living God . . . But with whom was he grieved forty years? was it not with them that had sinned, whose carcasses fell in the wilderness? And to whom sware he that they should not enter into his rest, but to them that believed not? So we see that they could not enter in because of unbelief."** (Heb. 3:12,17-19) **"But there were false prophets also among the people, <u>even as there shall be false teachers among you</u>, who privily shall bring in damnable heresies, even denying the Lord that bought them, and bring upon themselves swift destruction."** (II Pet. 2:1) The Word continues to say that many will follow their evil twisting of the Truth and through **"covetousness shall they with feigned words make merchandise of you."**

The warnings and standards by which we should evaluate those who are, in Truth, in the pulpits of our churches, those highly-ordained positions according to God, are clearly repeated throughout the Old and New Testaments. **"Know ye not that the <u>unrighteous</u> shall not inherit the** kingdom of God? **Be not deceived: neither** fornicators, nor idolaters, nor adulterers, nor effeminate, nor abusers of themselves with mankind, Nor thieves, nor covetous, nor drunkards, nor revilers nor extortioners, **shall inherit the kingdom of God.**" (I Cor. 6:9,10)

As written in the Scriptures, they may say: **"Lord, Lord, have we not prophesied in thy name? and in thy name have cast out devils? and in thy name done many wonderful works?"** But God rejects such "works of the flesh" as he did his once-chosen prophet of "old," Balaam: **"I never knew you: depart from me, ye that work iniquity."** (Matt. 7:22,23) "I tell you, I know you not whence ye are; depart from me all ye workers of iniquity." (Luke 13:27) "They profess that they know God; but **in works** they **deny him,** being abominable, and disobedient, and unto every good work reprobate." (Titus 1:16) It is stated that men will become **"lovers of their own selves, covetous, boasters, proud, blasphemers, disobedient to parents, unthankful, unholy, without natural affection, trucebreakers, false accusers, incontinent, fierce despisers of those that are good, Traitors, heady, high-minded,** lovers of pleasures more than lovers of God; Having a **form** of godliness, but denying the power thereof: **from such turn away.**" (II Tim. 3:2-5) God further describes these people who are headed toward eternal destruction: **"having eyes full of adultery, and that cannot cease from sin;** beguiling unstable souls; (because they have) **a heart they have exercised with covetous practices;"** (II Peter 2:14.) God calls them **"cursed children which have forsaken the right way and are gone astray."**

How do we know those who are preaching Truth? Measure messages taught by what the Word says. Investigate the lifestyles of those to whom you are listening. **"Wherefore by their fruits ye shall know them."** Man confuses fruit of the Spirit with works of the flesh. The two are clearly delineated in Galatians 5. **"Now the works of the flesh are manifest, which are these; adultery, fornication, uncleanness, lasciviousness, idolatry, witchcraft . . . heresies, envyings, murders, drunkenness . . . of the which I tell you before, as I have also told you in time past, that they which do such things shall not inherit the kingdom** of God. But the <u>fruit of the Spirit</u>, is love, joy, peace, long-suffering, gentleness, goodness, faith."

Those in leadership are to strictly follow Biblical standards just as every other man and woman on this earth must if s/he is to be saved. In both I Timothy, Chapter Three and Titus, Chapter One, the Lord clearly states specific requirements of those in church leadership:

1. They are to be the husband of one wife.
2. Their children should be in order.
3. Their wives should be faithful in all things.
4. They must rule their own house well.

Why are the standards for this particular profession specifically outlined? Man's theology reflects his morality: What a person teaches will be reflective of what is in his heart: **"But those things which proceed out of the mouth come forth from the heart; and they defile the man. For out of the heart proceed evil thoughts, murders, adulteries, fornications, thefts, false witness, blasphemies."** (Matt. 15:18,19) **"Keep thy heart with all diligence; for out of it are the issues of life."** (Pro. 4:23) God knows that man will speak and teach what is on the inside of him. If he lives in sin or approves of it, his "nature" will gravitate toward the seeking of like opinions either by identifying with those who agree or by the creation of like-mindedness in those under his care or sphere of influence.

We would not want a professional murderer, or thief, or prostitute to lead us in worship every Sunday morning. Most people would not accept the rationale justifying these peoples' sins. We know that **"out of the abundance of the heart the mouth speaketh,"** and that messages taught by such transgressors would be cloaked in deception. (Matt. 12:34) Likewise, one would need to listen carefully to the teachings of a pastor or other church leader who is not in a one-flesh marriage. Could he, **in Truth**, from what is in his heart, tell others he believes that marriage is "until death do you part - for better or for worse"? Can those whose households are not in order, properly counsel, in

Truth and with proper Biblical principles and authority, those who want out of a marriage or who have unruly children? God's word gives a negative answer. In His wisdom in setting standards for church leadership, He knew this. We need only to look to the Old Testament example from which the Lord may have drawn this prohibition for today's church leadership.

God's chosen people of "old" had prophets and priests who did the very thing that some leaders in the churches today are mirroring. "Sheep" were led into destruction just as they are being "beguiled" today. The record of God's response is in Jeremiah for us to study: **"Mine heart within me is broken, because of the prophets . . . the land is full of adulterers . . . both prophet and priest are profane; yea, in my house have I found their wickedness, saith the Lord . . . I have seen also in the prophets of Jerusalem a horrible thing: they commit adultery, and walk in lies: they strengthen also the hands of evil doers, that none doth return from his wickedness."** (Jer. 23:9-14) They taught people to sin by their examples and encouraged transgressors to continue in their wicked ways by approving of their iniquities. Why would they adopt any "better" behavior than their leaders? After all, the priests and prophets were "getting away" with their sins. Why should they be any different than their teachers? God destroyed both the leaders <u>and</u> those who permitted themselves to be led astray.

The Lord has not changed his standards. He gives man no excuse for rejecting what is commanded . . . **"Ordain elders in every city, as I had appointed thee: If any be blameless, the husband of one wife, having faithful children, not accused of riot or unruly."** (Titus 1:5,6) **". . . A bishop then must be blameless, the husband of one wife, vigilant, sober, of good behavior, given to hospitality, apt to teach; not given to wine, no striker, not greedy of filthy lucre; but patient, not a brawler, not covetous; one that ruleth well his own house, having his children in subjection with all gravity."** The Lord then tells very succinctly why this should be so: **"(For if a man know not how to rule his own house, how shall he take care of the church of God?) . . . Likewise must the deacons be** grave . . . Let the decons be the husbands of one wife, ruling their children and their own houses well." (I Tim. 3:2-5;8,12)

Are there churches which have in leadership men who are not the husband of one wife? Are there men in leadership whose children are unruly? We know the answer is affirmative. Does this mean that God approves? No, as with murder, stealing, or any other work of the flesh, God does not approve. He can only warn us to flee from being "beguiled" by such persons. The book of Jude gives final warnings: **"But, beloved, remember ye the words which were spoken before of the apostles of our Lord Jesus Christ; How that they told you there should be mockers in the last time, who should walk after their own ungodly lusts. These be they who separate themselves, sensual, having not the Spirit."**

Does church doctrine promote Biblical Truth?

In researching church doctrines on the issue of divorce and marriage the author will share with the reader the evolution of today's standards adopted by most of the churches in America. As Joseph Webb in his book, Till Death Do Us Part? remarks: "What we have seen happen in our churches has been a gradual change of attitude that has evolved over a period of many years. It has been said that 'backsliding is never a blowout, but just a slow leak.'"* (3:159) The church doctrine discussed below is that of a large nationwide denomination but is common to many. No attempt here is made to identify the denomination as the purpose is not to discredit any body of believers but to bring about an awareness of how the slight alteration of Biblical truths eventually brings massive destruction.

---

*The above book is available from Webb Ministries, Inc. Box 729, Longwood, FL 32750. The subtitle of this Biblically-based text is What the Bible Really Says About Marriage, Divorce, and Remarriage."

Adam and Eve violated this principle in the garden of Eden when the serpent said: **"Ye shall not surely die"** - if you disobey just a small portion of God's word! Man's sin nature mirrored rebellion throughout the Old Testament and continues today often cloaked under the heresy of false godly love and grace, especially with the sin of adultery.

In 1872, and previous to that date, the church doctrine referenced specifically for this discussion makes no mention of divorce in the section "Rules Relating to Marriage." Those married by clergy were to be saved Christians. Scripture quoted was that of II Corinthians 6:14. **"Be ye not unequally yoked together with unbelievers: for what fellowship hath righteousness with unrighteousness? and what communion hath light with darkness?"*** Mention was made that many who had rebelled against this Scripture by marrying unbelievers had themselves subsequently "turned away from the Lord and back to perdition." Women were instructed not to marry without the consent of their parents. It appears that the church's "foundation" was initially grounded on Scriptural principles.

In 1892, is the first mention of the approval of divorce: "divorce for adultery is 'lawful.'" No minister, however, was to solemnize any marriage in any case where there was a divorced wife or living husband . . . but the "innocent" party, if adulterous behavior of a mate had been proven, was permitted to marry a second partner. Repeated was the rule that the woman was to have the consent of her parents before marrying. The reference was again made to II Corinthians 6:14 regarding being equally yoked.

In 1900, the Scripture reference to II Corinthians 6:14 was omitted as was the rule for consent of parents before marriage.

In 1940, the church had maintained its regulation

---

*This Scripture is a **forewarning** from the Lord. It does not "release" a person from a life-time one-flesh covenant with a mate should there be changes in the state of the salvation of either spouse.

regarding the prohibition of ministers from solemnizing a marriage between divorced parties unless one of these was an "innocent" party via proven adulterous behavior by a mate. If either of the persons coming before the minister had a living mate who had not committed proven adultery, clergymen were still specifically prohibited from performing a ceremony. Satan had given man many years to "accept" the heresy that it's okay to change the rules just a little bit. But decay not removed will consume every part it touches. The "innocent party" exemption now becomes expanded to include others than the partners of sexually unfaithful mates. To the "established" departure from Biblical Truth was added other "exceptions" which the church said "invalidated the marriage vow." Included in the list of acts which now "invalidated" the marriage vow were "adultery or other vicious conditions which included mental or physical cruelty."

In 1952, the above rules were carried forward but a warning was added that violation of the "established" rules would be deemed an act of "maladministration."

In 1960, ministers were instructed to hold premarital conferences with the perspective bride and groom and to emphasize the spiritual values involved in all phases of marital and parental life of the marriage. Ministers were to likewise make this counseling available to those whose marriages were breaking down. With all the stated concern for the family unit, ironically another section of the **protective wall** for the institution of marriage is cleverly removed through the deception of the "Trojan Horse." Study the cover of this book and visualize God's highest church officials excitedly pulling this destructive animal into His most Holy institution! This was the year, 1960, in which the church officials completely removed the "adultery exception" for those who came before a minister to be married to a different mate. The change in church position was "cloaked" in the "humanistic" clause: "In view of the seriousness with which the Scriptures and the Church regard divorce . . . " Now clergymen could marry one-flesh spouses to other mates: if the divorced person was "sufficiently aware" of the factors leading to the failure of the previous marriage; if the divorced person intended to make a <u>second marriage</u> "truly Christian"; if a sufficient time had lapsed for counseling and preparation. However, no time period was defined to fulfill the requirement of "sufficient time."

In 1976, even the above stipulations were omitted. Included were several statements regarding the importance of the family unit to society and that the church does not recognize a relationship between two persons of the same sex as constituting marriage. The doctrine now stated stated that "when partners after thoughtful consideration and counsel are estranged beyond reconciliation, that it recognizes the right of divorced persons to remarry." The document expressed concern for the needs of the children. The seventies was the decade of the institution of No-fault Divorce legislation across our entire nation. The churches set the stage; millions have responded to be a part of the "cast!" We can see that what the church has year by year done in moderation, society has mirrored in excess until today the average person's heart is hardened against the reception of Biblical Truth regarding the marriage-covenant. Has God tragically turned America with our "reprobate" minds over to the desires of the flesh to let us continue in the sins we so openly promote?

On an individual basis, Joseph Webb, pastor of a church congregation discusses what has happened within the church itself in response to the changing doctrine of church leadership. Again from his text, <u>Till Death Do Us Part?</u>, this author writes:

> Several decades ago the church experienced an influx of couples who had been divorced and remarried. These couples had remained with their present partners for an extended period of time before they entered the church doors. Therefore, to make an issue of their present long term relationship caused much dissent in the churches by well-meaning church goers. The defenders of these couples said that the church should 'learn to forgive,' and not to treat these unfortunate people as 'second-class citizens.' That term,

'second-class citizens' became the offensive phrase and buzz word around which supporters rallied. A real struggle ensued, and no one came forth with a strong doctrinal position on this issue because it was so volatile. One needs only to examine most commentaries pastors use today and he'll find those passages that deal with divorce and remarriage were and are virtually skipped over, or very lightly touched upon.

The result of this compromise in the church reads like the parable of the Arab's camel. Remember, how the camel stuck his nose in the Arab's tent and asked, 'May I just keep my nose inside the tent to keep it warm?'

When given approval the camel stuck his whole head into the tent and asked if it was all right to keep his ears warm because it was so cold outside. The evident end of the parable was that inch by inch the camel moved into the tent until he was all the way in, and the Arab was out. It happened slowly, but it happened.

Likewise, through compromise and faulty doctrine, the camel of adultery is not only in the tent (the church), he has now made it easier for more camels of unrighteousness to enter into the tent.

It is time to recognize that divorced and remarried persons are not 'unfortunate or second-class persons.' They are sinners who sometime in the past made a quality decision to break a clear command, and who now need to repent that they may receive eternal life. Just because they are in denominational bodies does not mean they are in Christ. But the real tragedy is that they are not only **IN** churches, but occupy very influential offices in the churches as deacons, trustees, teachers, and pastors.

The Body of Christ must pay a dear price today if they would get the camel back out of the tent, and re-establish righteousness. But whatever the price, it is worthwhile to purify the assembly and to enlighten these dear sincere souls of their lost condition before it's too late. (3:159,160)

What does the Bible say will happen to those who continue to reject Biblical Truth?

We like to hear of the love of the Lord, of how he blesses people and cares for them, of how He forgives seventy times seven. But there is a side of God that man does not like to recognize - that of righteous judgment for sin, the payment of the **wages** for transgressions: the reaping of eternal punishment for unrepented rebellion. Most people have heard of a place called Hell. Many dispute the reality of it. Horror movies cannot begin to depict what Scriptures speak as Truth . . . there is a place of eternal torment for those who choose to continue in rebellion rather than to submit to obedience:

"**And if thine eye offend thee, pluck it out: it is better for thee to enter into the kingdom of God with one eye, than having two eyes to be cast into hell fire: where their worm dieth not, and the fire is not quenched.**" (Mark 9:47,48)

"**The worm shall feed sweetly on him; he shall no more be remembered.**" (Job 24:20)

"**The wicked shall be turned into hell, and all the nations that forget God.**" (Psa. 9:17)

"**Her house is the way to hell, going down to the chambers of death.**" (Pro. 7:27)

"**Even as Sodom and Gomorrah, and the cities about them in like manner, giving themselves over to fornication and going after strange flesh, are set forth for an example, suffering the vengeance of external fire.**" (Jude 7)

"In flaming fire taking vengeance on them that know not God, and that obey not the gospel of our Lord Jesus Christ: Who shall be punished <u>with everlasting destruction</u>." (II Thess. 1:8,9)

"And in hell he lift up his eyes, being in torments . . . have mercy on me . . . for I am tormented in this flame." (Luke 16:23, 24)

"The Son of man shall send forth his angels, and they shall gather out of his kingdom all things that offend, and them which do iniquity; And shall cast them into a furnace of fire: <u>there shall be wailing and gnashing of teeth</u>." (Matt. 13:41,42. See also Matt. 8:12; 13:50; 22:13; 24:51; 25:30; Luke 13:28)

Man cannot outguess God. The Lord treats everyone the same in terms of "qualifications" for the kingdom. **"The soul that sinneth, it shall die."** (Ezek. 18:20) But, we know not at what point in our lives that the Lord will say, "I've had enough with that person." God is **"long-suffering that none should perish,"** but we know that man does perish, as in the days of Noah when everyone except Noah and his family were destroyed. The Pharaoh was given ten opportunities to turn to the Lord. He with many followers perished. We know that Anannias and Sapphira lied to God about the price of a piece of land that they sold, and they immediately died. We know that God had mercy upon David in his sinfulness in committing an act of adultery and that David suffered through the rebellion of his children.

God's judgment on a high priest and judge over Israel was different than that experienced by David. Eli was a favored priest and was noted to have been a righteous man, but his sons **"knew not the Lord."** The violation of Biblical principles by this high priest and his sons brought righteous judgment - the **wages** of sin - unto his entire household. Eli, a church leader did not "rule his house well," and his sons, a part of the priesthood, greatly blasphemed the Holy Ghost.

Eli's sons seduced women who came to the temple for the purpose of giving their sacrifices to the Lord. Phinehas and

Hophni also took offerings which did not belong to them. As recorded, "**they lay with the women that assembled at the door of the tabernacle of the congregation.**" Eli told his sons that for the sin of robbing the offerings, he could judge them but for their sins of the flesh only God could so do: "**If one man sin against another, the judge shall judge him: but if a man sin against the Lord, who shall entreat for him?**" (I Sam. 2:25)

These vile men had wives of their own and as members of the household of the high priest were afforded a most comfortable standard of living, yet: "**When I had fed them to the full, they then committed adultery . . . They were as fed horses in the morning: every one neighed after his neighbor's wife.**" (Jer. 5:8) Phinehas and Hophni were warned that because of their great transgressions "**the Lord would slay them.**" Instead of punishing his sons, Eli unfortunately only reproved them. His warnings did not pierce their lustful hardened hearts and reprobate minds. "**They hearkened not to their father.**" They had long before established a pattern of rebellion against God's laws and may have had a contemporary attitude that they were "getting away" with their adultery; while instead, they were reaping the beginning stages of the **wages** of sin: hardened hearts, seared consciences, reprobate minds, and the withholding of the gift of grace. They not only sinned but caused others to transgress in that they "**caused many to stumble at the law.**" (Mal. 2:8) They corrupted the marriage-covenant and defiled the temple of the Holy Ghost.

Another principle that God perhaps tries to teach us by sharing this regrettable tragedy is that He does not treat all transgressions alike even though the final wage for sin is death. As with David, God remarked, "**because by this deed thou hast given great occasion to the enemies of the Lord to blaspheme, the child also that is born unto thee shall surely die.** (II Sam. 12:14) Additionally, we see here as in other Scriptures that sexual perversion is a sin directly against the body of Christ. "**Every sin that a man doeth is without the body; but he that committeth fornication sinneth against his own body. What know ye not that your body is the temple of the Holy Ghost.**" (I Cor.

6:18,19) Man can be punished by man for other sins, but **"whoremongers and adulterers, God will judge."**

The Lord's judgment came unto this entire household: **"For I have told him that I will judge his house for ever for the iniquity which he knoweth; because his sons made themselves vile, and he restrained them not."** (I Sam. 3:31) Not only were those immediately involved affected by these transgressions but generations thereafter were so recorded. A short time after the warning from God both Phinehas and Hophni were killed - on the same day, followed shortly thereafter by the death of their father; he who had power to restrain the sins of his sons but made himself partaker in the guilt, became an "accessory" to their transgressions.

Phinehas' wife was reported to have been grieved over the death of her husband and father-in-law. She was pregnant at the time and shortly thereafter delivered her child, a son. Whether she died as a complication of child birth or of a broken heart, her dying comments were a lament for the sins against the Lord: **"The glory is departed from Israel: because the ark of God was taken, and because of her father-in-law and her husband. And she said, The glory is departed from Israel: for the ark of God is taken."** (I Sam. 4:21,22)

"Today if ye will hear his voice, harden not your hearts." (Heb. 4:7)

People across our nation who truly wish to stop the rampant destruction must start with a heart desire to repent. It does not matter whether we have been directly involved in the sin of adultery, or if we have been an "accessory" by encouraging others to enter into such a relationship, or in some other manner been a participant in **"putting asunder what God hath joined together."** (Matt. 19:6) As members of the body of Christ, as parents and grandparents of the next generation, can we expect young adults to believe us if we tell them that marriage is until death if we are holding the hand of a non-one-flesh mate? Can clergymen who marry mates to a second spouse, explain to God their Biblical Truth for performing "adulterous ceremonies" and officiating over second vows from participants who have already made previous vows before God and a covenant with Him and another mate - "until **death** do us part"? Children learn what they live. Is it too late to save the family in America?

> "<u>If</u> my people, which are called
> by my name,
> shall humble themselves, and pray,
> and seek my face, and <u>turn</u> from their wicked ways;
> <u>then</u> will I hear from heaven, and will forgive their
> sin, and will heal their land."
> (II Chr. 7:14)

Begin now to "renew" your mind by memorizing Scriptures that our nation may be healed from destruction from within. A "starter dough" is given on the following page. Comb this text and the Scriptures for verses which confirm God's commands regarding His institution of marriage.

GOD'S WILL AND COMMANDS FOR MARRIAGE

I, ( ), take thee, ( ), to be my wedded husband/wife, to have and to hold, from this day forward, for better, for worse, for richer, for poorer, in sickness and in health, to love and to cherish, <u>till death us do part</u>, according to God's holy ordinance; and thereto I plight thee my faithfulness.

I resolve to: **"be not conformed to this world: but be transformed by the renewing of my mind, that I may prove what is that good, and acceptable, and perfect, will of God.** (from Rom. 12:2)

"This is <u>now</u> bone of my bones, and flesh of my flesh." (Gen. 2:23)

"And unto the married I <u>command</u>, yet not I, but the Lord, Let not the wife depart from her husband: But, and if she depart, let her remain unmarried, <u>or</u> be reconciled, to her husband: and let not the husband put away his wife." (I Cor. 7:10,11)

"<u>Whosoever</u> shall put away his wife, <u>and</u> marry another, committeth adultery against her. And if a woman shall put away her husband, and be married to another, she committeth adultery. (Mark 10:11,12)

"For the woman which hath a husband is bound by the law to her husband so long as he liveth; but if the husband be dead, she is loosed from the law of her husband. So then if, <u>while her husband liveth</u>, she be married to another man, she shall be called an adulteress: but if her husband be dead, she is free from that law; so that she is no adulteress, though she be married to another man." (Rom. 7:2,3)

"But <u>whoso</u> **committeth adultery with a woman** (man) **lacketh understanding: he** (she) **that doeth it <u>destroyeth</u> his** (her) **own soul."** (Pro. 6:32)

CHAPTER 9
WHAT DOES OUR GOVERNMENT SAY ABOUT MARRIAGE?

"Woe unto them that decree unrighteous decrees
and that write grievousness which they have prescribed."

"Anything which overturns the order or system of things whereby families are destroyed and the whole of society adversely affected is by definition a catastrophe." (4:1) This author, an attorney from Texas, J. Shelby Sharpe, has been a forerunner in the legal arena in the struggle against the destruction of the family unit. In his paper, "NO-FAULT DIVORCE - A NATIONAL CATASTROPHE," Mr. Sharpe continues by outlining the devastation created by the destruction of over a million families every year since 1970. This was the year when the Uniform Marriage and Divorce Act was passed by the National Conference of Commissioners on Uniform State Laws. "Today," says, Mr. Sharpe, "all fifty states have some form of this statute." (4:2) This attorney could find no instance when a divorce was denied to the petitioning party under the present guidelines included in the statutes. What the "system" used as a premise on which to pass such a law was the "inevitability of divorce"; therefore, "the procedures should be changed to minimize the amount of damage to the parties and their children following the divorce . . . Tragically, history has shown that the change to a no-fault system instead of solving the problems of troubled marriages has only exacerbated the problems like pouring gasoline on a small fire." (4:2)

Attorney Sharpe gives us some insight regarding the direction that No-fault is and has been taking us. He, too, quotes from Dr. Etzioni's testimony before the United States' sub-committee on Family and Human Services regarding the Oversight on the Breakdown of the Traditional Family Unit: "Dr. Etzioni testified that at the current rate of divorce there would not be a family left untouched by it in America by the year 2008." As noted in Chapter Eight of this book, Dr. Etzioni referred to No-fault Divorce as "mail-order" destruction of the family unit. Mr. Sharpe adds to this: "It is significant to note that one of the first things V. I. Lenin did when he came to power in the Soviet Union after the Revolution in 1917 was to have passed what amounts to our no-fault divorce statutes. Lenin, and later Stalin, determined that in order to maintain control of the people it would be necessary to completely destroy the family and restructure it. Thus, on September 16, 1918, a law was passed whereby one could obtain a divorce by simply mailing or delivering a postcard to the local registrar without the necessity of even notifying the spouse being divorced." One only needs to comb the law books in America to find that this is indeed happening in America. In some courts divorces are being granted without jurisdiction being established and in others without the opposing spouse even being represented in court.

How has a country established on Biblical principles gone so far awry? Review the preceding chapter of this book. We saw that the church once upheld the Biblical law of marriage, but year by year eliminated just a "tittle" until today all that is left is what will "tickle" man's ears: "Where marriage partners, even after thoughtful consideration and counsel, are estranged beyond reconciliation, we recognize divorce as regrettable but recognize the right of divorced persons to remarry. We express our deep concern for the care and nurture of the children of divorced and/or remarried persons . . . We encourage an active, accepting, and enabling commitment of the church and our society to minister to the members of divorced families." The "world" has only mirrored what the churches in the beginning allowed in moderation but turned to excess.

As mentioned in earlier chapters of this text,

corruption which <u>creeps</u> into any ordinance of God must be purged by going back to its origin. Adulterated versions must be eliminated. Truth is **"from the beginning"** and not in the permissions, tolerations, and allowances given to rebellious, sinful man. Even in the legal and political arena we can trace the origins of our foundations and see that what we have "touted" as "Constitutional" is as far from truth as is what is being "touted" as Truth in the churches!

What is secular humanism?

The judicial system's solution to solving man's desire for "happiness," "with no consequential responsibility," has been the passage of a law which says that no one is at fault and the courts will dissolve, in man's eyes, a marriage with or without the consent of the other spouse. There is no recognized legal defense for the Defendant (Respondent) which will stop such an action by the state to use its Trojan Horse, No-fault Divorce, to pronounce its death sentence upon the institution of marriage. This popular way of dealing with sin today has evolved through the legislation of principles from the religion of secular humanism. This includes adoption of "fairness laws" which justify sin. It tries to remove guilt by doing away with God's standards. It says no one is at fault. Along the same line of thinking is the judicial system's pretense that we can't legislate morality. This is false. Every law legislates morality - God's or man's. It is impossible to be religiously or morally neutral. If a political system rejects one authority, it adopts another. If a Biblically moral system is rejected, an immoral system is substituted. No-fault encourages Biblical adultery. What if we turned the tables and determined to discourage this behavior? What if we "exhorted" spouses to work problems out by replacing our current divorce legislation with the Old Testament Mosaic law of stoning to death all adulterers and adulteresses? We know, however, that this, too, would be non-Biblical -- but probably would slow the rate of divorce!

Secular humanism is the established religion in our

schools and rules over most of our nation. This religion denies God, Christ, and basic Christian principles. It was given legal sanction in the case Torcaso v. Watkins, 367 U.S. 488 (1961). From that time on there has been a tidal wave of non-Christian rulings permeating every part of our nation.

The doctrines behind what we have become as a nation under humanism should be carefully studied. John Dewey, whom many educators honor as the "father of progressive education" drafted the initial Humanist Manifesto I. Charles Francis Potter, an honorary president of the NEA was one of the original signers of this document. From the Humanist Manifesto II, the following "affirmations" are summarized:

1. Faith in a prayer-hearing God is an unproved and outmoded faith. Reasonable minds look to other means for survival.

2. Traditional moral codes and messianic ideologies cannot cope with existing world realities.

3. Examples of humanism which need to be implemented include free thought, atheism, Marxist humanism. (The author of It's A Matter of Life or Death adds that the Soviet Union and China are two countries whose economic theories are based upon Marxism. Not many people in the United States have a desire to live in either of these countries, yet we are adopting little by little, the "foundations" of these systems.)

4. Humanists state that there is insufficient evidence for belief in the existence of a supernatural being. They call themselves non-theists and state that no deity will save them; they must save themselves.

5. Humanists view immortal salvation or fear of eternal damnation as illusionary and harmful as they "detract humans from present concerns."

6. They believe that moral values and ethics should be based upon spontaneous and situational circumstances and there is no substitute for reason and intelligence. (Thus, we see in our

classrooms moral absolutes of the Bible being replaced with "values clarification" and "situational ethics" in which students may be given mock problems to solve with choices among solutions which include all non-Biblical responses. In selecting one of the given answers the student becomes "right" by choosing something which is Biblically immoral/wrong.)

7. All religious or moral codes that suppress freedom of choice are rejected.

8. They believe that orthodox religions unduly repress sexual conduct; they foster the "right" to abortion and divorce and that the many "varieties" of sexual exploration should not in themselves be considered "evil." Individuals should be permitted to express their sexual "proclivities" and pursue their life-styles as they desire. Parochial loyalties and inflexible moral and religious ideologies should be done away with.

9. They strongly favor one-world government and the elimination of disparities of income between peoples.

10. "The separation of church and state are imperatives."

There is little doubt that Dewey with his influence through the National Education Association utilizing the "medium" of professional educators, mastered the technique of "teaching" not only children but also adults most of the above list. With the **"protective wall"** of Biblical principles abandoned in large part by the church, seeking individuals have like the Arab invited the camel into the tent and have permitted the camel to push out Godly principles. Let's take a closer look at the last tenet of secular humanism, the separation of church and state.

What does "separation of church and state" mean?

Think how you would answer the following questions? Perhaps you might even want to write your answers on paper so that you can refer back to them after reading the remaining portions of this chapter.

1. What was the purpose for which our country was founded?
2. What did our founding fathers have to say about Christianity?
3. What is the Magna Carta?
4. Where is the phrase "separation of church and state" found?
5. Do our foundational documents tell us that the church is to be separate from the state?
6. Who wrote the phrase "separation of church and state"?
7. Is the government supposed to protect our religious rights?

The purpose for which our country was founded was twofold:

1. for the glory of God
2. for the advancement of the Christian faith

How do we know that to be true? Look at the next page. On it you will find a portion of The Mayflower Compact dated 1690. Notice the underscored portion for emphasis. The people who signed this document gave up material possessions, friends, and family ties to establish our country. They did so because of their beliefs in God as their creator and Jesus Christ as their Savior. As stated, their religion was Christian.

A document from which many of our judicial principles were adapted was the Magna Carta. This British document was also soundly grounded on Biblical precepts. "Know that, having regard to God and for the salvation of our soul, and those of all our ancestors and heirs, and unto the honour of God and the advancement of holy Church . . . In the first place we have granted to God, and by this our present charter confirmed for us and our heirs for ever that the English church shall be free, and shall have her rights entire, and her liberties inviolate; and we will that it be thus observed" (emphasis added). This document was based upon:

1. an allegiance to God

THE MAYFLOWER COMPACT
1690

In the Name of God, Amen. We, whose names are underwritten, the Loyal Subjects of our dread Sovereign Lord King James, by the Grace of God, of Great Britain, France, and Ireland, King, Defender of the Faith, &c. Having <u>undertaken for the Glory of God</u>, <u>and Advancement of the Christian Faith</u>, and the Honour of our King and Country, a Voyage to plant the first colony in the northern Parts of Virginia . . . in the <u>presence of God</u> . . . <u>covenant</u> and combine ourselves . . . for Furtherance of the Ends aforesaid . . .

FIRST AMENDMENT TO THE
CONSTITUTION OF THE UNITED STATES

Congress shall make no law respecting an establishment of religion, or prohibiting the free exercise thereof . . .

CONSTITUTION OF THE SOVIET UNION

"In order to ensure to citizens freedom of conscience, <u>the church in the U.S.S.R. is separated from the State, and the school from the church.</u> . . " (Article 124)

2. the protection of the Christian church

3. protection of civil liberties through <u>procedural due process</u> - rights to be protected according to law or through proper legal procedure. (What has evolved today is called <u>substantative due process</u>, law "interpreted" with personal bias according to current value systems based upon what is "reasonable" at a particular time.)

The Pilgrims and our forefathers, including Washington, Jefferson, and even Benjamin Franklin, all had very evident in their writings an allegiance to God and the Christian faith. We see repeatedly references to men who knew God and the importance of **"Except the Lord build the house, they labor in vain that build it."** (Psa. 127:1) This included not only the home, but church, school, state and national government.

In the Northwest Ordinance we find "<u>Religion</u>, <u>morality</u>, and knowledge . . . being necessary <u>to</u> good government <u>and</u> the <u>happiness of mankind,</u> <u>schools</u> and the means of education . . . shall forever be encouraged." It would probably be quite a shock to those who formulated the Northwest Ordinance to find that in this great country of ours it is now illegal to have prayer as part of the daily classroom procedure; the Ten Commandments can no longer be displayed; moral absolutes of the Bible are being replaced by values clarification and situational ethics. These men would find the teaching of Christian principles in our public schools largely replaced by those of secular humanism. They would find evolution taught to the exclusion of creationism. They would find professional educators persecuted for reading from the Bible in our public schools, while peers read freely from and teach other non-Christian doctrines.

Further evidence of the original Godly intent of our founders and framers of our foundational documents is so overwhelmingly clear - if we would only **"study to show ourselves approved . . . rightly dividing the word of truth."** (II Tim. 2:15) Many readers are familiar with our Liberty Bell Pavilion in Philadelphia. There is housed our Liberty Bell. Inscribed upon this historical symbol is a permanent record of the intent of the framers of our foundational documents: **"Proclaim liberty throughout all the land unto all the inhabitants thereof."** This inscription on the Liberty Bell is from the Bible. You can read it for yourself in Leviticus 25:10.

Further reference to Leviticus is the honoring of the Lord one day a week. This for most Christians has been designated as Sunday. We see reference to this holy day in Article 1, Section 7 of the Declaration of Independence: "If any bill shall not be returned by the President within ten days (Sundays excepted) . . ." This reference is in keeping with the command in Leviticus: **"keep my sabbaths, and reverence my sanctuary: I am the Lord."** Those who study the Word know that man is told that his land will be blessed: **"If ye walk in my statutes, and keep my commandments, and do them."** (Lev. 26:2,3) Congress began its sessions with Divine worship, and many presidents have declared national days of prayer and fasting.

Reach into your pocket and pull out a coin and a Federal Reserve Note. On the face of every coin, you will find inscribed "In God we Trust." Likewise on the back of every Federal Reserve Note, you will find "In God we Trust" (emphasis added).

The "separation of church and state" is one of the most misinterpreted non-Biblical phrases in our country. Citizens from grade-school age through adulthood have been "taught" that this directive is written in the First Amendment to our United States Constitution. Refer again to page 149 where this amendment is given: "Congress shall make no law respecting an **establishment** of religion, or **prohibiting** the free exercise thereof." Two commands are given to Congress:
1. Congress is not to establish a religion or to make a law respecting such.
2. Congress is not to prohibit anyone from practicing his/her religion.

The religion referred to by the Pilgrims was definitely that of Christianity. Many of the aforementioned symbols, documents, and founding principles were assuredly Christian based. The intent, which has been almost completely aborted, was to prohibit the establishment by Congress of a new national religion and that all persons should be equally

entitled to the protection of their religious liberties.
Nowhere in the First Amendment
1. is there any phrase which says there is to be a separation of church and state
2. is there any phrase which even mentions "church"

Perhaps one of the problems is that man has lost his reference to some basic terms regarding church and religion. In the Supreme Court opinion of Justice Field in which polygamy was outlawed, the following definition of religion was given. "The term religion has reference to one's views of his relation to his creator, and to the obligations they impose of reverence for his being and character, and obedience to his will." (Reynolds v. United States 98 U.S. 145 [1878])

Church and religion are not synonymous terms. Church is the physical building or body in which a religion is housed. The term, church, to non-Christians, is a physical building. Christians take their definition from the Bible which tells us that as believers we are a part of the body of Christ: **"Christ is the head of the church."** (Eph. 5:23) Religion is a collection of beliefs generally based upon what exists beyond the visible world. Christians believe that God is the creator and controller of the universe and everything in it. In its original state it was perfect. Man, placed upon the earth with a free will, has always had the option of choosing between good and evil. He, in choosing evil, has perverted himself and much of what God intended to work for good within his life. Man has an innate desire to be a god and in such a state develops an uncontrollable lust for power, possessions, and personal gratification. We saw the beginnings of this with Adam and Eve in Chapter One of this book.

There is no clause in the United States Constitution against the establishment of religion or the protection of the established religion. What is prohibited is that **CONGRESS** is not authorized to establish a religion nor is it to prohibit people from practicing theirs. We did see earlier in this chapter in a court case that the judicial branch unconstitutionally "established" secular humanism as a religion (Torcaso v. Watins, 367 US 488 [1961]).

Many believe that Thomas Jefferson wrote the phrase, "separation of church and state," into our Constitution to separate church from the state. Thomas Jefferson did not sign nor draft the First Amendment. He was indeed a prolific writer and speaker, authoring some 25,000 letters and giving many speeches. This phrase has been improperly quoted (garbled) from a letter which Jefferson wrote to a group of clergymen. He was assuring them that there would never be the establishment of one <u>denomination</u> over another such as the Congregationalists over the Baptists. This has been used out of context and completely in opposition to the purpose for which it was written. Jefferson was close enough to the time and circumstances giving rise to the writing of the Declaration of Independence to know well the <u>protection</u> needed <u>from</u> an ungodly national power. "He [the king of Great Britain] has combined with others to subject us to a Jurisdiction foreign to our Constitution, and unacknowledged by our Laws; giving his Assent to their Acts of pretended Legislation . . ." (Declaration of Independence).

    The First Amendment was a part of an instrument to protect and perpetuate <u>already existing</u> religious values of this nation, not to destroy them. The men who signed this historical document so evidence their belief by a direct reference to the Lord, Jesus Christ: "Done in Convention, by the unanimous consent of the States present, the seventeenth day of September, **in the year of our Lord** one thousand seven hundred and eighty-seven" (emphasis added).

    This phrase, "separation of church and state" has been incorporated into our land, established to glorify God, from a nation which has as its goal to destroy the political system upon which America was formulated. From the Constitution of the Soviet Union, we read the directive that our judicial system is and has been using as a "Trojan Horse" to destroy our foundations: "<u>In order</u> to ensure to citizens <u>freedom of conscience</u>, the church in the U.S.S.R. is <u>separated</u> from the State, and the school from the church" (emphasis added). (See page 149.) Notice the contrast in purpose between the Constitution of the Soviet Union ("to ensure to citizens freedom of conscience") versus the purpose for which our country was founded ("for the glory of God, and Advancement of the Christian Faith").

How has No-fault legislation evolved?

Let's look at the decay of a legal system initially set up to protect and allow citizens to practice their religion to one that has turned its back on God. Just as the church has turned away from the Biblical meaning and understanding of marriage, so has our government. Civil laws were originally set up to protect the rights surrounding marriage and Godly principles. In a court case in 1913, it was clearly thus stated:

> All of the duties and obligations that have existed at any time between husband and wife existed between those husbands and wives **before** civil government was formed. The truth is that <u>civil government has grown out of marriage</u> . . . from which government became necessary to . . . protect the weak, and to conserve the moral forces of society, <u>to the support of religion</u> and free government (emphasis added). Grisby v. Reib, 105 Tex. 508, 153 S.W. 1129, [1913]

In attorney Sharpe's paper referenced earlier, he quotes from another case, Pappas v. Pappas, on the obligation of government to marriage:

> . . . the State and society have an interest in keeping intact all such contracts [marriage] and in protecting them to the fullest extent. (146 S.W. 2d 116)
>
> The Supreme Court of the United States in <u>Maynard v. Hill</u> characterized marriage as 'the most important relation in life,' and the foundation of the 'family and of society, without which there would be neither civilization nor progress.' 125 U.S. 205, 211. The court has reaffirmed this characterization and importance of marriage as recently as 1978 in Zablocki v.

Redhail, 434 U.S. 374.

Our courts long ago saw the devastation to society that would happen if easy divorce were permitted as is seen in <u>Sheffield</u>, where Chief Justice Hemphill observed that 'the prospect of easy separation foments the most frivolous quarrels and disgusts into deadly animosities.' 3 Tex. 86. His concluding remark was that when husbands and wives know they cannot end their relationship by mutual consent or for light or frivolous reasons, 'they become good husbands and wives; for necessity is a powerful master in teaching the duties it imposes.' 3 Tex. 86.

There has been a complete redefining of 'legal rights and responsibilities of husbands and wives.'[24] Marriage is protected by divorce laws.[25] However, <u>when the divorce laws change, the attitude of the courts toward protecting marriage changes</u>[26] (emphasis added). This is graphically seen in the language of the opinion in <u>Cusack v. Cusack</u>, to wit: 'Until 1969 . . . Texas legislation on grounds for divorce remained virtually unchanged for over a hundred years. The adversary nature of divorce litigation remained, and <u>ancient ecclesiastical grounds</u> for separation <u>based upon fault formed the core</u> of substantive divorce law . . It became apparent in the late 1960s that <u>existing grounds for divorce</u> and the <u>defenses</u> thereto were no longer compatible with modern beliefs.' [Emphasis mine] 491 S.W. 2d 716. **Thus, there is now no judicial protection for a spouse who desires to save a marriage** (emphasis added). (5:6)

Attorney Sharpe through his research reaffirms the fact "that the family existed 'before civil government was formed'" and that one of the primary responsibilities of civil government was the protection of this unit. The failure to do this has reaped "awesome consequences to take place." Mr. Sharpe continues "Because mankind is by nature lawless, civil government has as one of its foremost responsibilities the punishment of wrongdoers.[27]" (4:6) As Miss Decker stated in her testimony regarding the institution of marriage, man has reversed the basic purpose of our judicial system: "We are permitting ourselves to become a society that punishes the virtuous. That punishment is every day being incorporated into the laws of the land, written and unwritten." (See Chapter Eight.) No-fault Divorce legislation most assuredly punishes those who try to practice their religion and do what is "right" Biblically.

What is the relationship between church and state?

The court cases above have a striking parallel to the change in the attitude toward the protection of the family unit expressed by changing church doctrines. In 1960 the church eliminated the "adultery exception." In the case Cusack v. Cusack the following was noted: "It became apparent in the late 1960s that existing grounds for divorce and the defenses thereto were no longer compatible with modern beliefs (emphasis added) . . . When the divorce laws change, the attitude of the courts toward protecting marriages changes."

In the 1913 case of Grisby v. Reib, the following was stated: "The contract of marriage is the most important of all human transactions. It is the very basis of the whole fabric of civilized society." Hopefully the reader will see a very "subtil" error here. (The word "subtil" is chosen from Genesis 3:1 to make a point regarding the danger of not knowing Scripture: **"Now the serpent was more subtil than any beast of the field which the Lord God had made."** What was quoted above was "almost" correct. Certainly the attitude of the heart and what it basically said was correct. The "subtil" deadly error inserted and "made law" was the use of the word "contract." Marriage is not a contract; it is a covenant. Contracts, man has jurisdiction over; covenants are God's domain. Contracts can be and are broken, destroyed, made null. A marriage-covenant is only dissolved upon death of one of the partners. Man "knows" in his heart that marriage is for life but lacks "understanding," and thus we have highly intelligent people making ungodly, unconstitutional laws based on changing morality of man to regulate God's institution of marriage. As Attorney Sharpe comments.

> God says that His thoughts are not our thoughts and His ways are not our ways." [Isa. 55:8] He also tells us that there is 'a way which seems right to man, but its end is the way of death.' [Pro. 14:12] . . . To try to solve the problems we face with human wisdom is foolishness. [I Cor. 3:18,19]

Why is the No-fault Divorce law unconstitutional?

As you did with the section on separation of church and state, before reading this passage, how would you answer the following questions?
1. What is a contract?
2. What are the Constitutional protections of a contract?
3. What is the normal legal procedure for someone who breaks a contract?

There are many definitions of a contract but a simplified one would include an enforceable agreement between two or more competent persons embodying an offer by one person to do or not to do a particular thing and an acceptance by another. Certain things that are generally understood regarding contracts can be found in most law books: "An essential part of free enterprise in our economic system is that <u>the rights created by contracts are protected</u>. Each party must observe the terms of the contract, and generally <u>government cannot impair the obligations of a contract</u>. Economic life would be most uncertain and it <u>would be impossible</u> to plan ahead <u>if</u> we did not have the <u>assurance</u> <u>that agreements</u> <u>once made</u> <u>would be binding</u>" (emphasis added). (5:27)

The basis for our contractual law comes from our Constitution. The Fourteenth Amendment states: "No State shall make or enforce **any law** which shall abridge the privileges or immunities of citizens of the United States, nor shall any State deprive any person of life, liberty, or property without due process of law, nor deny to any person within its jurisdiction the equal protection of the laws."

In Article 1, Section 10 of the United States Constitution, the states are forbidden to pass any ex post facto law. Most state constitutions also contain similar prohibitions to guarantee the avoidance of such action by a legislative body. What this refers to is that it is unconstitutional to pass a law after the occurrence of a fact or an act which retrospectively changes the legal consequences or relations of such fact or deed. It in essence protects what was done "from the beginning, from the first act, from the inception" as is confirmed by Black's (law) Dictionary.

We also have protected civil rights contained in the Bill of Rights **guaranteed** to every citizen of the United States. These include freedom of religion, freedom of speech, the right to petition the government, freedom of one's house and person from unwarranted search and seizure, right to have legal assistance in one's defense, freedom from bills of attainder, freedom from ex post facto laws, freedom from cruel and unusual punishments.

Like the protection guaranteed by the United States Constitution ("Congress shall make no law respecting an establishment of religion, or prohibiting the free exercise thereof . . .") state constitutions have corresponding protections for its citizens. Contrary to these safeguards, No-fault Divorce statutes were enacted in most states in the 1970s. This Trojan Horse in 1987 issued the "death" sentence on some 1,157,000 family units. With 2.5 people per household this means that 2,892,000 lives were directly affected. Thousands immediately become financially disadvantaged and many psychologically damaged, especially children. In its movement to dispel "traditional" notions about divorce in both the religious and legal arenas -- making it "easier and less painful and to remove the stigma," our nation has taken a legal stand to depart from its Biblical heritage regarding the institution of marriage.

Our Judicial system's solution, supported by most "churches," for solving man's desire for "happiness" with no consequential responsibility has been the passage of a law which says that no one is at fault. It in reality <u>guarantees</u> a verdict for the Plaintiff: the person asking our judicial system to break his/her legally binding contract. The courts will dissolve, in man's eyes, a marriage with or without the consent of the other spouse with <u>no</u> recognized legal defense for a Defendant which will stop such an action by the state. The Plaintiff is only required by law to establish residency and to bring before the judge a corroborating witness for this purpose. Some courts assume jurisdiction without even satisfying this minimal legal requirement. The Plaintiff has only to state that the marriage is irretrievably broken and the judge raps his gavel: "verdict for the Plaintiff!" The destruction does not stop here. The "right" to divide children and property automatically follows. Already shared has been the testimony of witnesses regarding the horrible injustices psychologically to these innocent parties. Properties are taken against Respondents' permission and often without even a pleading for partition within the proceedings or legal briefs. The judicial system defines marriage as a contract but gives it none of the guaranteed Constitutional protections. In the absence of <u>any</u> criminal charges brought against the "innocent party," to give the state "just cause," civil protections and religious rights are denied.

Unique only to the marriage "contract" is that no one is held responsible and the party actually at fault may sue the "innocent" party for divorce and "win," and be absolved of paying thousands of dollars in legal fees for the "innocent" party who was forced into court against his/her will to defend a Biblical right (if a believing Christian). The Plaintiff is additionally rewarded for breaching the contract. The state, by man's law, dissolves a covenant (contract) into which it did not enter. A bilateral agreement is unilaterally dissolved without legal reasons having to be shown and their plausibility judged. In no other "contractual" situation are these exceptions made.

In contractual law, the party against whom the breach

has been committed is Constitutionally guaranteed the same legal recourse, rights, and Constitutional protections as does the party bringing the action. There are, however, no bilateral equal rights under No-fault, especially for the "minority sect" wishing to practice Biblical commands regarding God's institution of marriage. This statute flagrantly, "under color of the law," strips opposing parties of their civil rights and many of those guaranteed by the amendments to the Constitution.

Defying the prohibition against states imposing legal duties or privileges upon certain sects or classes of persons that are not imposed on others, the states, including the United States Supreme Court, practice legalized crime right in our halls of justice. Those opposing a dissolution, and especially on Biblical grounds, are most assuredly a "minority sect" with unrecognized rights, privileges, and immunities.

The "majority sect" is not only protected with guaranteed rights for a verdict in his/her favor but is additionally encouraged by the government to apply for an unconstitutional "mail order" divorce. The state rewards those consenting parties who want to dissolve a marriage, by providing preprinted forms. Parties desiring a divorce can simply go to the courthouse and purchase the complete "do-it-yourself kit." State employees will even assist "customers" in filling out the papers.

There is, however, no comparable "kit" available for those wishing to preserve a marriage. Instead cruel and unusual punishment is inflicted. Indigents are forced into court against their will and required to go deeply into debt to hire a lawyer. If the latter becomes impossible, and they attempt to represent themselves, the judicial system has erected a legal wall that makes it almost impossible for a Defendant to survive. State employees refuse to answer any questions or offer assistance. The Defendant, untrained in legal matters, is forced to file papers and write briefs following state and federal rules of civil procedure - an impossibility for most. The ability to "petition the government," a guaranteed civil right, is denied such incompetent indigents, "under color of the law."

Constitutional protections provided under the ex post facto provision are denied. Those married before the passage of this No-fault legislation should be protected from having "contracts" dissolved because of the provisions of this law, but again, the tyranny against the breakdown of the family is never ending. All marriages come under the law established by God before any civil law! The judicial system including the United States Supreme Court and the lower courts have been vested with the duty to interpret the Constitution under the framework in which it was created. Justices, judges, and officials of the courts are making law rather than interpreting what has been established in light of historical facts and the language and intent of those who wrote our legal framework. Procedural due process has become a substantative tool which adept attorneys and judges manipulate against weak and unprotected, financially handicapped Defendants forced into court against their wills to defend the family unit. (Please read Psalm 119:126.)

Given in summary form below are our judicial system's overt actions to destroy the institution of marriage. These are done "under color of the law" in a nation whose originating purpose was "for the glory of God and Advancement of the Christian Faith."

> 1. It is matter of fact and law that our judicial system flagrantly discriminates against parties contesting divorce actions.
> 2. It is a matter of fact that the state will act and issue decrees and orders when it does not have jurisdiction of the subject matter and of the parties.
> 3. It is a matter of fact and law that our judicial system violates ex post facto protection afforded by Article 1, Section 10 (retrospective laws) in dissolving marriages under the No-fault Divorce law.
> 4. It is a matter of fact and law that in the absence of any criminal charges, pleadings, etc. our judicial system, with its tyrannical power, will divest a person of marital status, moneys, properties, and

family, violating inalienable rights of life, liberty, and property.

5. It is a matter of fact and law that the government treats the marriage-covenant as a contract but does not afford the "minority sect" rights to protect this contract.

6. It is a matter of fact and law that the government in treating the marriage-covenant as a contract does not afford Defendants equal protection concerning Article 1, Section 10 regarding the passage of any law impairing the obligations of contracts; that is, the Constitutional guarantee that laws may not be passed which impair obligations or performance of obligations of contracts.

7. It is a matter of fact that indigents are deprived equal access to courts and equal legal representation because of expenses required to retain legal representation and thus become unprotected incompetents without a guardian or means to "redress the government for grievances."

8. It is a matter of fact and law that the judicial system has unconstitutionally established a monopolistically discriminatory sect - those filing a suit to dissolve a marriage - and awards to it rights and privileges not afforded Defendants in the minority sect - those objecting to a dissolution of marriage.

9. It is a matter of fact that the judicial system will unconstitutionally deny access to the court to an indigent and leave such Petitioner legally unprotected without Due Process of law; will refuse right of appeal to same; will refuse to forward appeals properly filed by an indigent forced to act for self, and manipulate away basic civil rights to such an unprotected incompetent.

10. It is a matter of fact and law that the

judicial system provides forms, formats, and aid by state employees for parties who agree to a divorce but discriminates against incompetent indigent Defendants. These are instead forced to follow the Federal Rules for Civil Procedure, Rules of the Supreme Court of the United States, etc. - an impossibility for most lay persons.

11. It is a matter of fact that the judicial system is abandoning procedural due process and promulgating substantative due process by using personal bias to interpret what it considers within its present value system as "reasonable."

11. It is a matter of fact and law that our judicial system is "under the color of the law," serving as a catalyst to obtrusively and tyrannically destroy the family unit in America.

The above observations are made from the point of view of a lay person but certainly warrant some second thought. It's not difficult to see that our judicial system not only does not understand the marriage-covenant but that it also "garbles" the meaning of a contract when applied to marriage. It places a Christian Defendant in a pseudo-double jeopardy denying the right of protection of religious commands regarding the institution of marriage and in defining marriage as a contract likewise denies other Constitutionally guaranteed protections and civil rights.

In Chapter Four, the reader was warned against being "beguiled" within the church by **"false teachers among you, who privily shall bring in damnable heresies, even denying the Lord that bought them."** (II Peter 2:1) The example of twisting and misusing Scripture out of context was given with that of Judas: **"And Judas went out and hung himself . . . Go therefore and do likewise . . . And do so quickly."** (Matt. 27:15; Luke 10:37; John 13:37) We know full well that Truth is not told by joining these three Scriptures. This same procedure in the legal arena called garbling has been used to deceive this nation regarding the sanctity of

163

marriage by turning the very documents set up to "glorify God" and "advance the Christian faith" into religious persecution by our judicial system to destroy our foundation - the family unit.

With only the "marriage contract" do the parties not know what the terms will be years from when they entered into the binding agreement. In <u>Economics of Divorce</u> by Lenore J. Weitzman, she reported that 100 percent of respondents to a survey indicated they believed their marriage would be a life-long partnership in which they would share all acquired property and income, in all tangible and intangible aspects." (6:1249) "Whereas the traditional law sought to deliver a system of moral justice and which rewarded the 'good' spouse and punished the 'bad' one, the no-fault law ignores the spouses' moral history . . ." (6:1186) Attorney Sharpe contends that "No court should ever be permitted to grant a divorce contrary to the vows of the parties. **The parties have the right to know the basis upon which their marriage stands.** Civil government should support rather than destroy attendant rights pertaining to this voluntary covenant of the parties as to the duration of the marriage and agreed upon grounds for dissolution; e.g. 'until death we do part.'" (4:9)

There is an answer to all the destruction in America. Go back to the beginning. Examine our foundational documents as they were written and within the context for which they were formulated. Let us be a nation under God. Purge the "ungodly copies" remembering the permissions, tolerations, and allowances given to deal with rebellious, sinful man are not Truth to be adapted as Biblical guidelines and lifestyles. In referencing the "beginning" of the civil arena recall Chief Justice Brown's statement regarding the fact that marriage was not originated by human law.

> All of the duties and obligations that have existed at any time between husband and wife existed between those husbands and wives before civil government was formed. The truth is that civil government has grown out

of marriage.

Return again to the Declaration of Independence to observe the close parallels regarding America's treatment of those whose "duty" to their God is to defend their rights to Biblical principles and especially those regarding God's institution of marriage. Where the reference to the king of Great Britain is written, insert our judicial system.

> The History of the present King of Great Britain is a History of repeated Injuries and Usurpations, all having in direct Object the Establishment of an absolute Tyranny over these States. To prove this, let Facts be submitted to a candid World.
>
> He has refused to Assent to Laws, the most wholesome and necessary for the public Good.
>
> He has combined with others to subject us to a Jurisdiction foreign to our Constitution, and unacknowledged by our Laws; giving his Assent to their <u>Acts of pretended Legislation</u> (emphasis added).
>
> For protecting them, <u>by a mock Trial</u>, from Punishment for any Murders which they should commit on the Inhabitants of these States (emphasis added).
>
> For depriving us, in many Cases, of the Benefits of Trial by Jury.
>
> For taking away our Charters, abolishing our most valuable Laws, and altering fundamentally the Forms of our Governments.
>
> In every stage of these Oppressions we have Petitioned for Redress in the most humble Terms: Our repeated Petitions have been answered only by repeated Injury. A Prince, whose Character is thus marked by every act which may define a Tyrant, is unfit to be the Ruler of a free People.
>
> . . . We have reminded them of the

Circumstances of our Emigration and Settlement here. We have appealed to their native Justice and Magnanimity, and we have conjured them by the Ties of our common Kindred to disavow these Usurpations, which, would inevitably interrupt our Connections and Correspondence. They too have been deaf to the Voice of Justice and of Consanguinity.

We, therefore, the Representatives of the UNITED STATES OF AMERICA, in General Congress, Assembled, appealing to the <u>Supreme Judge of the World</u> for the Rectitude of our Intentions . . ." (Declaration of Independence) (emphasis added).

In America, we have a Godly heritage as exhibited by the creators of the Mayflower Compact. Those who established our country did so in honor of Him who created them and us: "In the Name of God, Amen. We, whose names are underwritten . . . <u>Having undertaken</u> **for the Glory of God,** and **advancement of the Christian Faith** . . . a Voyage to plant the first colony in the northern parts of Virginia; Do by these Presents, <u>solemnly and mutually</u>, **in <u>the presence of God</u>,** and one another, **covenant and combine ourselves together into a civil Body Politick, for** our better Ordering and Preservation, and Furtherance <u>of the Ends aforesaid</u>" (emphasis added). Our judicial system not only breaks - in man's eyes - the <u>covenant</u> between one-flesh relationships but also that between the founders of our country and God. We have been blessed beyond what most of us deserve, yet we have turned from God. We have pulled the Trojan Horse into our homes, our church assemblies, and our halls of justice. We have allowed and are encouraging the seeds of destruction. Even though God warns: **"Woe unto them that decree unrighteous decrees and that write grievousness which they have prescribed,"** man appears to have lost the fear of the other side of our loving Father, Creator, and Savior. He is also a just, jealous, and wrathful God. The author ends this chapter with a final plea in quoting with permission from an article from <u>Herald of His Coming</u>, called "False Security" by Greg Hinnant. Mr. Hinnant uses a somewhat different system of citations which are not explained within the article. Any questions relative to this article can be addressed to the above publication Box 886, Newton, Kansas 67114. The author will add emphasis by underscoring and with bold highlighting. (7:1,11)

For an ungodly people, there is no security in having a godly heritage. 'Sin is a reproach to any people,' and that includes God's very own **covenant** people (Pr. 14:34). God plays no favorites; He judges sin, regardless of where He finds it. The spiritual descendants of the saintliest saints are not safe from the righteous judgment of God if they themselves turn away from Him . . .

Before Zephaniah's time, Jerusalem and Judah had been a center of righteousness, the very dwelling place of God. Many godly men called Jerusalem home . . . Holy prophets by the score had lived there. No place on earth had a richer spiritual heritage than did Jerusalem, the holy city. It had been the most favored spot, hand-picked by the Almighty. Surely, therefore, God would never judge Jerusalem!

Yet He did just that! All the righteousness of Judah's great spiritual heritage could not prevent the wrath of a holy God from falling upon the holy land, which had become quite unholy.

After years of its enjoying a peaceful but false security, God's righteous judgment finally came upon Jerusalem, <u>as prophesied</u>. The incredible, the unthinkable, the unbelievable happened. Vile Nebuchadnezzar's armies besieged, then took, the city of Jerusalem for the Second and final time.

'And they burned the house of God and

broke down the wall of Jerusalem, and burned all its palaces with fire, and destroyed all its precious vessels. And those who had escaped from the sword carried he away to Babylon, where they were servants to him and his sons . . . to fulfill the word of the Lord by the mouth of Jeremiah . . .' (2 Chr. 36:19-21; Amos 2:4,5).

AMERICA, BE NOT DECEIVED!

America is also under the spell of a false security. 'O foolish Americans, who hath bewitched you that ye should not obey the truth?' (Cp. Gal. 3:1) Many American Christians mistakenly imagine that because this country was founded by a remnant of righteous men, that God will surely pass over our sins in this day and spare us severe judgment.

But He will not. Without **repentance,** this country, as Judah of old, is headed for future shock. **The Pilgrims and the Puritans were pure in Christ Jesus;** twentieth century Christianity, as it is generally practiced in the United States, is far from it. Only 'righteousness exalteth a nation . . .' (Pr. 14:34).

God makes no promises to arrogant sinners and careless Christians. Our spiritual heritage assures us of nothing. The Lord seeks current righteousness from this generation of believers, not a lot of puffed up, pious talk about those who founded this country, godly though they were. Many of us are bloated with a sickening sense of pride in our religious heritage. And God Himself, not the devil, is determined to deflate us.

'Sin is a reproach to **any** people,' and every generation that sins will reap the due measure of punishment that they deserve (Cp.

Pr. 11:31b; Gal. 6:7). Their punishment will not be lessened by the fact that they had in fact a godly heritage. If anything, it will be worse -- 'For unto whomsoever much is given, of him shall be much required' (Lk. 12:48; Cp. Amos 3:2)." (7:1,11)

Return unto the Lord with all your hearts!
(I Sam. 7:3)

SCRIPTURE VERSES TO RENEW MY MIND

"Woe unto them that decree unrighteous decrees, and that write grievousness which they have prescribed."(Isa. 10:1)

"Woe to them that devise iniquity, and work evil upon their beds! when the morning is light, they practice it, because it is in the power of their hand. And they covet fields, and take them by violence; and houses, and take them away: so they oppress a man and his house, even a man and his heritage." (Micah 2:1,2)

". . . if ye do return unto the Lord with all your hearts, then <u>put away</u> the strange gods . . . from among you, and prepare your hearts unto the Lord, and serve him only." (I Sam. 7:3)

"It is time for thee, Lord, to work: <u>for they have made void thy law</u>." (Psa. 119:126.)

"Ye shall keep my sabbaths, and reverence my sanctuary: I am the Lord. If ye walk in my statutes, and keep my commandments, and do them; Then I will give you rain in due season, and the land shall yield her increase, and the trees of the field shall yield their fruit." (Lev. 26:2,3)

" . . . proclaim liberty throughout all the land unto all the inhabitants thereof." (Lev. 25:10)

"Except the Lord build the house, they labor in vain that build it." (Psa. 127:1)

- - - - - - - - - - - - - - - - - -

Congress shall make no law respecting an establishment of religion, or prohibiting the free exercise thereof . . .
First Amendment to the Constitution of
The United States of America

CHAPTER 10
WHAT IF...?

This book was written to share a Truth about marriage that man today rejects - that **marriage is for life** upon this earth. When a person goes to the altar, the commitment is made not only to that person who will become a one-flesh mate for life but . . . to God. Many approach the altar as born-again, spirit-filled, Bible-committed Christians. We have seen, however, that even with these, **"some shall depart from the faith . . . they shall turn away their ears from the truth."** Your one-flesh mate has a free will. S/he can leave you, can refuse to provide for you, can have an affair, can physically or mentally abuse you. That is why you must realize that **your covenant is unconditional.** It ultimately is based on a relationship with Jesus Christ, and His Word is the **"same yesterday, and today, and for ever."** The Lord honors your marriage-covenant as long as both you and your one-flesh mate are living here on this earth. There are no other conditions. (We did see that in I Corinthians 7 that a provision has been made for spouses to live separately if that becomes necessary.)

For our protection of the family unit, God has provided a **"wall"** based on Biblical Truth to surround the institution of marriage. This **"wall"** is intangible. It is a system of beliefs that we have a choice of accepting or rejecting. Summarized in the typical marriage vows are the foundation blocks which, if properly used and cemented together with agape love, will be impenetrable by any destructive influence. There must be a conviction within the heart by both parties to build this **"wall"** based on Biblical principles. Each must make a firm commitment to God's unchanging position that the marriage-covenant is until death - for better or worse. That's the decision necessary to ward off the Trojan Horse of destruction in your home.

Man has now built into our current judicial system one of history's most destructive weapons ever devised for the destruction of marriage, No-fault Divorce. It is time for people to take a stand for Biblical Truth if our nation is to survive. That resolve must start with individuals who have a desire to see a turn-around in our nation, in our homes, in each person who has turned from the Lord. It must begin with you and with me.

It does not matter what you have done (save blasphemy of the Holy Spirit). **If** you truly repent, turn from what God calls sin, He will forgive. You can be clean and pure in His eyes. We must daily search our lives as to whether we are or whether we are not following Biblical principles by **"rightly dividing the word of truth."** However, even though we turn from sin, there may be a great price to pay as we live out our days on this earth. There is a sowing and reaping. Sin has its price! But, it's better to pay now than to spend an eternity in torment . . . for the **"wages of sin is death."**

God's agape love is tied to grace. We <u>may</u> have a second, or third, or fourth chance with all sin. We, however, do not know how many chances before God will say He's had enough. Eli, as well as his sons, were destroyed because this father did not follow Biblical principles in reproving his children. David suffered the consequences of his one specific act of adultery for the rest of his days on this earth. The Pharaoh was given ten chances before the Lord destroyed him and his followers in the Red Sea. Ananias and Sapphira lied to God one time - at least that is the only record we have of this couple's sin. Their lives were taken almost immediately. We must not mistake God's patience as approval of sin. Its intent is for all to repent and thus be saved through His grace from eternal damnation.

It doesn't take a fancy prayer to make a commitment to the Lord, just an honest desire to make the Word of God first place in your life. It is, however, a two-way partnership. God doesn't force you. He is always there, but you must do your part. His promise is "draw nigh to me, and I will draw nigh to you." "Hunger and thirst after righteousness, and you shall be filled." You can simply say, "God, please help me. I am miserable; I can't help myself. I want to stop committing sin in my life. I acknowledge You as my Lord and Savior. Help me to have a desire for Your Word and a true relationship with You." **"Seek ye first the kingdom of God, and his righteousness; and all these things shall be added unto you."** (Matt. 6:33) **"Delight thyself also in the Lord; and he shall give thee the desires of thine heart. Commit thy way unto the Lord; trust also in him; and he shall bring it to pass."** (Psa. 37:4,5)

Find a church that teaches Truth from the Scriptures. Attend church regularly where you can learn Truth, and spend time praising and worshipping the Lord. Daily read and <u>study</u> the Bible for yourself. Fellowship with Christians who encourage Biblical principles.

Meditate on these closing words written by Paul: **"For I am jealous over you with godly jealousy: for I have espoused you to one husband, that I may present you as a chaste virgin to Christ. But I fear, lest by any means, as the serpent beguiled Eve through his subtilty, so your minds should be corrupted from the simplicity that is in Christ."** (II Cor. 11:2,3)

What if . . . our judicial system "by consent" continues to encourage the destruction of over one million family units per year?

. . . "And this shall be a sign unto you, saith the Lord, that I will punish you in this place, that ye may know that my words shall surely stand against you for evil . . . Shall not my soul be avenged on such a nation as this? (Jer. 44:29;5:9)

What if . . . Joseph and Mary had said: "I can't believe God would really want us to bear this child and suffer all the ridicule surrounding these circumstances; and, besides, who will miss one baby 2,000 years from now?"

. . . Hundreds of prophecies contained in the Old Testament would not have been fulfilled through Joseph and Mary. Jesus Christ would not have entered the world to provide the Way, the Truth, and the Light for us. What God proclaimed in Genesis would not have been Truth. **"Before I formed thee in the belly I knew thee; and before thou camest forth out of the womb I sanctified thee . . . "** (Jer. 1:5)

What if . . . man persists in twisting Biblical truth?

. . . "And for this cause God shall send them strong delusion, that they should believe a lie: That they all might be damned who believed not the truth, but had pleasure in unrighteousness." (II Thess. 2:11,12)

What if . . . The government issues you or your spouse a divorce decree, or a church gives you an annulment, and you marry another spouse?

". . . <u>Whosoever</u> putteth away his wife, and marrieth another committeth adultery; and <u>whosoever</u> marrieth her that is put away from her husband committeth adultery." (Luke 16:18)

"So then, if <u>while her husband liveth, she be married to another man, she shall be called an adulteress.</u>" (Rom. 7:3)

. . . "And I gave her space to repent of her fornication; and she repented not. Behold, I will cast her into a bed, and <u>them that commit adultery</u> with her into great tribulation, <u>except</u> they repent of their deeds." (Rev. 2:20-22)

"Though it be but a man's <u>covenant</u>, yet <u>if it be confirmed</u>, <u>no man</u> disannulleth, or addeth thereto." (Gal. 3:15)

What if . . . John the Baptist had not told King Herod that marriage to someone who already had a living one-flesh mate was wrong in God's eyes?

. . . God would not have had a witness to tell non-Christians that they, as well as Christians, are held responsible regarding God's prohibition against a second marriage if <u>either</u> of the parties has a living one-flesh mate. "<u>**Whosoever** </u>**putteth away . . .**" (Luke 16:18)

What if . . . Noah had said: "God may have said that I needed to build a boat, but I have been ridiculed for 119 years with no rain and none in sight. I have this ark, 450 feet long, 75 feet wide, and 45 feet high, sitting in my front yard with no humanly perceptible means of using it. I'm tired of being the laughing stock of my neighborhood."

. . . His family would not have been saved. **"By faith Noah, being warned of God of things not seen as yet, moved with fear, prepared an ark . . . to the saving of his house."** (Heb. 11:7) Was it worth it for Noah to persevere?

What if . . . Jesus had told the Pharisees to stone the woman caught in adultery?

. . . God would have re-established the Mosaic line of punishment for men and women today. Everyone who commits adultery or fornication, physically or mentally, would be stoned to death. Thousands of men and women would be stoned every day in the United States and other countries. **"but thou hast played the harlot with many lovers; <u>yet return again to me, saith the Lord.</u>"** (Jer. 3:1)

What if . . . man sins just a little, tells a few lies, looks at another person with lust in his heart . . . ?

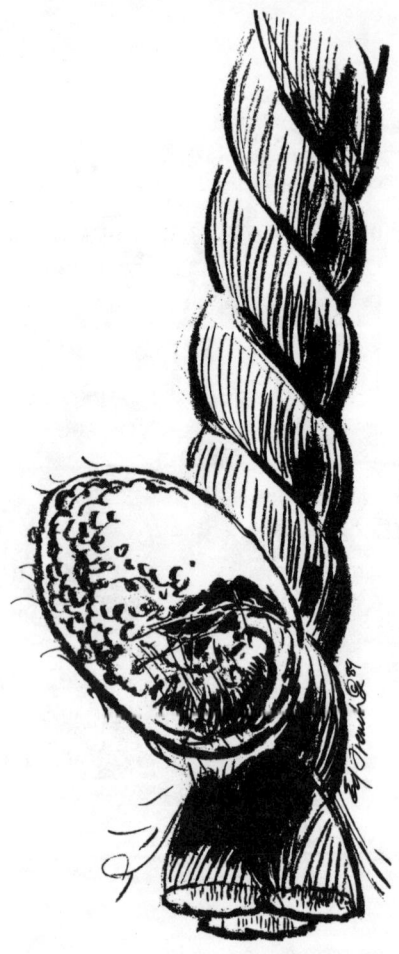

"Then when lust hath conceived, it bringeth forth sin: and sin, when it is finished, bringeth forth death." (Jas. 1:15)

"While they promise them liberty, they themselves are the servants of corruption: for of whom a man is overcome, of the same is he brought in bondage." (II Pet. 2:19)

". . . be not entangled again with the yoke of bondage." (Gal. 5:1)

What if . . . a person should die without repenting of fornication, adultery, stealing . . . ?

Be not deceived: neither fornicators . . . nor adulterers . . . nor thieves shall inherit the kingdom of God." (I Cor. 6:9,10) "And these shall go away into everlasting punishment: but the righteous into life eternal." "But unto them that are contentious, and do not obey the truth, but obey unrighteousness, indignation and wrath, Tribulation and anguish, upon every soul of man that doeth evil." (Matt. 25:46; Rom. 2:8)

What if . . . Jesus had said: "Everyone, even my disciples, have deserted me. It appears that you, God, have forsaken me too. You surely wouldn't expect me to endure the pain of these nails in my hands and feet. I've changed my mind. I did nothing to deserve this kind of treatment. I would like to have you take me down from this cross."

. . . None of us would have a sacrifice for our sins. We would be under the Old Testament "justification" and would have to sacrifice animals every day for the sins that we commit by word, thought, or deed. Instead, "**God so loved the world, that he gave his only begotten son, that whosoever believeth in him should not perish, but have everlasting life.**" (John 3:16)

What if . . . I have a sincere desire in my heart to repent and to seek the kingdom of God and His righteousness?

"Have mercy upon me, O God according to thy loving-kindness: according unto the multitude of thy tender mercies blot out my transgressions. Wash me thoroughly from mine iniquity, and cleanse me from my sin. For I acknowledge my transgressions: and my sin is ever before me. Against thee, thee only, have I sinned, and done this evil in thy sight . . . Behold, thou desirest truth in the <u>inward</u> parts: and in the hidden parts thou shalt make me to know wisdom. Purge me with hyssop, and I shall be clean: wash me, and I shall be whiter than snow. Make me to hear joy and gladness . . . Create in me a clean heart, O God; and renew a right spirit within me. Cast me not away from thy presence; and take not thy Holy Spirit from me."

(Psa. 51:1-4,6,7,8,10,11)

SCRIPTURE VERSES TO RENEW MY MIND

"Have mercy upon me, O God according to thy loving-kindness: according unto the multitude of thy tender mercies blot out my transgressions . . ." (Psa. 51)

"For God so loved the world, that he gave his only begotten Son, that <u>whosoever</u> believeth in him should not perish, but have everlasting life." (John 3:16)

"By faith Noah, being warned of God of things not seen as yet, moved with fear, prepared an ark to the saving of his house; by the which he condemned the world, and became heir of the righteousness which is by faith." (Heb. 11:7)

"Fear the Lord, thy God, to keep all his statutes and his commandments . . . and <u>thou shalt teach</u> them <u>diligently</u> unto <u>thy children</u>, and shalt talk of them when thou sittest in thine house and when thou walkest by the way, and when thou liest down, and when thou risest up." (Deu. 6:2,6,7)

"Know ye not that the unrighteous shall not inherit the kingdom of God? Be not deceived: neither fornicators, nor idolaters, nor adulterers nor effeminate, nor abusers of themselves with mankind, Nor thieves, nor covetous, nor drunkards, nor revilers, nor extortioners, shall inherit the kingdom of God." (I Cor. 6:9,10)

"For John had said unto Herod, It is not lawful for thee to have thy brother's wife." (Mark 6:18)

"And for this cause God shall send them strong delusion, that they should believe a lie: That they all might be damned who believed not the truth, but had pleasure in unrighteousness." (II Thess. 3:11,12)

"They were as fed horses in the morning: every one neighed after his neighbor's wife. Shall I not visit for these things? saith the Lord: and shall not my soul be avenged on such a nation as this? (Jer. 5:8,9)

BIBLIOGRAPHY

1. U.S. Government, <u>Broken Families: Hearings before the Subcommittee on Family and Human Services of the Committe on Labor and Human Resources United States Senate Ninety-eighth Congress First Session on Oversight on the Breakdown of the Traditional Family Unit, Focusing on the Causes and Implications for Society and the Role of Government in Helping Prevent the Breakup of Families</u>, (Part 2) September 22 and October 4, 1983.

2. U.S. Government, <u>Broken Families: Hearings before the Subcommittee on Family and Human Services of the Committe on Labor and Human Resources United States Senate Ninety-eighth Congress First Session on Oversight on the Breakdown of the Traditional Family Unit, Focusing on the Causes and Implications for Society and the Role of Government in Helping Prevent the Breakup of Families</u>, (Part 1) September 22 and October 4, 1983.

3. Webb, Joseph A., <u>Till Death Do Us Part? What the Bible Really Says About Marriage, Divorce and Remarriage</u>, Webb Ministries, Inc. P.O. Box 729 Longwood, FL 32750.

4. Sharpe, J. Shelby, "NO-FAULT DIVORCE - A NATIONAL CATASTROPHE," (unpublished paper).

5. Anderson, Ronald A. and Walter A. Kumpf, <u>Business Law Principles and Cases</u>, South-Western Publishing Co, Cincinnati, 1958.

6. Weitzman, Lenore J., <u>The Economics of Divorce: Social and Economic Consequences of Property, Alimony and Child Support Awards</u>, (Reprinted from UCLA LAW REVIEW Volume 28, August 1981, Number 6 by Lenore J. Weitzman).

7. Hinnant, Greg, "False Security," <u>Herald of His Coming</u>, Gospel Revivals, Inc. P.O. Box 886, Newton, KS 67114, June 1989.

ADDITIONAL SCRIPTURE VERSES TO RENEW MY MIND

MY PRAYER LIST

NOTES

NOTES

NOTES

ANOTHER AVAILABLE PUBLICATION

WITH THIS RING I THEE WED is a unique Biblical study of the marriage-covenant and vows starting with that original ceremony in the garden of Eden between God and Adam and Eve. Discussed are the following: Who created the institution of marriage? Who or what is it that marries a man and woman? What is love? Included is a copy of "The Order for the Solemnization of Matrimony" with keyed points of emphasis highlighted for discussion throughout the text.

This manual is designed not only for those who engage in pre-marital counseling - to give to brides and grooms, but also for those who are already married to review the commitments to which they have agreed. This one-of-a-kind marriage manual is written in a straight-forward style. It is easy to read and understand.

A better wedding card for the bride and groom could not be had. Some may wish to present a copy to everyone in the wedding party or even to each guest who comes to the marriage ceremony. The cover stock of **WITH THIS RING I THEE WED** is a beautiful mauve hue with gray print serving as a background for the decorative wreath surrounding the title. The quiet beauty of the cover is carried into the text by the use of a soft gray-tone paper and ink.

If you have read **IT'S A MATTER OF LIFE OR DEATH,** you may recognize the above synopsis. **WITH THIS RING I THEE WED** is Chapter Two of the aforementioned book with only the illustration on page twenty-four omitted. Added is a registration page to permanently record the members of the wedding party.

By Judith A. Brumbaugh

WITH THIS RING

I THEE WED

THE MARRIAGE-COVENANT AND VOWS

WHAT DO THEY MEAN

THE DOVE

"And Jesus, when he was baptized, went up straightway out of the water: and, lo, the heavens were opened unto him, and he saw the Spirit of God descending like a dove, and lighting upon him: And lo a voice from heaven, saying, This is my beloved Son, in whom I am well pleased." (Matt. 3:16,17)

The dove, a symbol of the Holy Spirit, also represents gentleness and innocence. It is defenseless, faithful to its mate, and home-loving. This same bird was sent forth by Noah from the ark: **"Also he sent forth a dove from him, to see if the waters were abated from off the face of the ground."** (Gen. 8:8)

ORDER FORM
COMMITTEE FOR THE RESTORATION
OF THE FAMILY

(Box 1342 Oviedo, FL 32765)

DESCRIPTION	QUANTITY DESIRED	PRICE EACH	TOTAL COST
IT'S A MATTER OF LIFE OR DEATH WRONG THINKING ABOUT MARRIAGE LEADS TO DESTRUCTION! (Add $1 for shipping and handling.)		$7.00	
WITH THIS RING I THEE WED THE MARRIAGE-COVENANT & VOWS WHAT DO THEY MEAN (Add 50¢ for shipping and handling.)		$3.00	
Florida residents only, add 6% sales tax to price of books ($7.21; $3.18).	SUBTOTAL		
	SHIPPING & HANDLING		
	TOTAL		

Prices are subject to change without notice. (Outside U.S., add $4 for shipping and handling.)

CHECK ENCLOSED IN THE AMOUNT OF _____.

NAME   (Please print.)

STREET ADDRESS   (Please print.)

CITY   STATE   ZIP   (Please print.)

Allow three to four weeks for delivery.

ABOUT THIS BOOK . . .

IT'S A MATTER OF LIFE OR DEATH: WRONG THINKING ABOUT MARRIAGE LEADS TO DESTRUCTION is a one-of-a-kind book which combs the Scriptures in a unique study of the vows and marriage-covenant. Never before have Biblical principles on the foundation of the family been so clearly and frankly discussed and graphically illustrated in one text.

This book is a teaching anthology based upon lives in the Bible to develop an understanding of how God looks at marriage, starting with that first marriage ceremony in the garden of Eden between Adam and Eve and God. Included is an in-depth study of what the marriage-covenant and vows mean.

Each of the illustrated ten chapters concentrates on the varied misunderstandings that have developed through the ages about the permanence of the marriage-covenant. Additional research reveals the changing attitudes of the church and government toward marriage and their roles as catalysts in the breakdown of the family unit. The unconstitutional aspects of No-fault Divorce are examined as applied to Christian marriages and the related controversy of separation of church and state.

This is a text every Christian should study. Each person married or anticipating such a commitment ought to carefully examine the generic aspects of this comprehensive, unique work. Parents will want their children to read this book before they enter into a marriage. Sound Biblical principles are clearly presented in a teaching style that makes the reader want to delve even deeper into the essentials of a Godly home.